FELHES
.40.5342
W

FEI
CW00693160

To Mum

you do find

strange things on

Amazon.

love
Jane.

C0000 002 188 135

CORDUROY DAYS

First edition, published in 2000 by

WOODFIELD PUBLISHING
Woodfield House, Babsham Lane, Bognor Regis
West Sussex PO21 5EL, England.

© Josephine Duggan Rees, 2000

All rights reserved.
No part of this publication may be reproduced
or transmitted in any form or by any means,
electronic or mechanical, nor may it be stored
in any information storage and retrieval system,
without prior permission from the publisher.

ISBN 1-873203-48-9

C2 188 135 01105

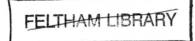
FELTHAM LIBRARY

HESTON LIBRARY.

Corduroy Days

JOSEPHINE
DUGGAN REES

Woodfield Publishing
BOGNOR REGIS • WEST SUSSEX • ENGLAND

The Author – at farm billet, Fawley 1940.

Contents

The Author (right) in 1941 at Brockenhurst with a fellow Land Girl.

Preface

This book is an account of my varied experiences in the Women's Land Army in the County of Hampshire from June 1940 to September 1944. Some of the names have been deliberately altered, a few I have forgotten.

For information about the Land Army in general I am indebted to Vita Sackville-West's book *The Women's Land Army* published in 1944 by the Ministry of Agriculture and Fisheries and to the magazine of the W.L.A. *The Land Girl*.

Humorous episodes from the original script of *Corduroy Days* have appeared as articles in *The West Sussex Gazette* and *Hampshire* the county magazine.

Josephine Duggan Rees
March 2000

Girls in WLA uniform at a prize-giving in 1941.

CHAPTER 1

Volunteering

The two girls in front of me were volunteering for the WAAF, the three at the back of the queue were, I decided, potential WRENS, while the whispered conversation of the little bunch in between divulged that they were intent on joining the ATS. On the other side of the room a silent line of young men were joining up in H.M. Forces.

It was September 1939, a week after war was declared and we were assembled in the Scout Hut, commandeered as a Recruiting Centre, in the small, country town of New Milton in Hampshire.

The WAAFs had enrolled and gone. I moved up to the desk and the ATS volunteers crowded behind me. I alone seemed to be joining the Women's Land Army.

"The Land Army…", the recruiting officer repeated after me. She eyed me dubiously. I was of medium height but slight of build and did not, it seemed, conform to her idea of the ideal land worker.

"Are you certain you are making the right choice?" she asked.

"Absolutely certain." I replied, in a tone that could have left her in no possible doubt.

She frowned slightly and presented another difficulty.

"There is no demand for Land Girls at the moment" she said.

It seemed that although I was ready and eager for the land, the land was not ready to receive girls in brown corduroy and green Jerseys. It had not yet dawned upon the British farmer that in time, some of his labour would be supplied by women.

The WLA had been formed on 1st June that year and already there were over a thousand girls trained and ready for employment, but farmers were reluctant, even refusing to take them. Nevertheless, I left my name, address and age, (I was seventeen, the minimum age for the Land Army) and was advised to return to the job I was doing and wait. This, I learned, was the predicament of many girls who volunteered for the land early in the war, only to find themselves without a job for many months.

Sadly disappointed, I went back to the small, residential hotel in Bournemouth where I was training as a receptionist, to what now seemed the trivial tasks of typing menus, arranging flowers and attending to the wants and whims of the wealthy, elderly residents.

The proprietress, my employer, was more sceptical than the recruiting officer when I told her I was joining the Land Army. She threw back her carefully coiffured head and laughed.

"My dear you won't stick it a month!" she declared.

Even my mother puckered her brow and asked "But why the Land Army?"

"Why not?" I replied. "I've always wanted an outdoor life … and weren't we farmers way back? I'm sure I've seen a photograph of my grandmother milking a cow."

Although born and bred in a large town on the South coast, I had moved with my mother to the countryside near New Milton the previous year and taken to country life like a duck to water. I became obsessed with the desire to work in some capacity on a farm. Now, here was the great opportunity, tragic though the circumstances were that had brought it about. It had taken no more than a moment to decide that the regimented life of the Women's Forces was not for me. My personal contribution to the National effort was to be on the land.

Nevertheless, as the weeks passed, I ceased to watch daily for my call-up and more or less settled down to my former routine.

Bar the lurking apprehension of a nation at war, life went on much the same, except that we carried our gas masks out of doors and rationing began. The hotel residents, to whom mealtimes were the highlight of their monotonous days, stared in stunned disbelief at the tiny portions of butter and sugar carefully measured out by the head waiter. Blackout regulations were meticulously observed, the big windows of the lounge that looked out over the sea being checked with especial care.

The lifestyle of Bournemouth was little changed. There were still good plays at the Little Theatre and revues at the Winter Gardens, Skating had ceased at the Westover, but a dance floor replaced the ice rink and tea dances were held there as well as at the Pavilion. There was morning coffee at Beales and tea at the Cadena and beautiful things in the shops before the introduction of utility goods. But an hour's programme at the little News Theatre jolted one up-to-date with the hard facts of war; troops embarking 'somewhere' and wistful, wide-eyed evacuees arriving at their new homes.

There were preparations too, against enemy invasion. Signposts disappeared from all road junctions and even in the country, people filled and stacked sand bags, taped windows and made improvised air raid shelters. Air raid wardens were trained.

The weather those last months of the year was mild. I swam in the sea almost every day until mid-December, for the Bournemouth beaches were not barricaded and barbwired like those further east along the coast. However, after Christmas winter tightened its grip and in January heavy snow, icy winds and prolonged frost transformed the countryside.

"Aren't you glad you're not in the Land Army now"? I was asked continually. But I wasn't. I envied the few girls who were "in at the beginning", however severe the elements.

Meanwhile I had learned something of the organization of the Land Army. The headquarters, which at the outbreak of war had moved from London to the Sussex country mansion of Lady Denman, Hon. Director of the W.L.A., worked in close co-operation with the Ministry of Agriculture. It was staffed with representatives at County levels to whom each volunteer was just a number and list of statistics, down to area representatives, who got to know each girl personally, safeguarded her interests and well being and kept in touch with the farmers. They were sympathetic, motherly women who carried out their not always easy duties with tact and charm.

In the spring, my local representative, a Mrs Jenkins, came to see me at home on my weekly day off from the hotel. There was still no news of a job but she chatted about the land work over a cup of tea, and I signed a form to say that I would go willingly to any part of the country where labour was needed. This was a compulsory condition, but in Hampshire and other largely agricultural counties few girls were sent far from their homes, although girls from the industrial cities of the Midlands went to Kent and some from London to the most desolate hill farms in Wales, where many must have suffered loneliness and homesickness. I also had to produce a medical certificate to prove that I was physically fit for farm work.

This cosy interview differed from those in the towns, where girls had to appear before a committee and were scrutinised and questioned at some length on their suitability; in rural districts it was much less formal.

Spring, too, brought gloomy news from the continent. Lightning attacks by the Germans brought about the collapse of Holland, Belgium and Luxemburg. Neville Chamberlain resigned and Winston Churchill became Prime Minister; stirring messages in his resonant, magisterial voice came over the radio; then the enemy swept through France, splitting the Allied Forces.

Again, I contacted Mrs Jenkins in my anxiety to join in the war effort, only to be told once again to continue my present employment and wait.

I was still waiting when the war-torn remnants of an Army rescued from Dunkirk limped into the town. The sight of these gaunt, sunken eyed, nerve-racked men appalled the residents. Then the first bomb, dropped just off the Isle of Wight Needles, shook buildings at 2 o'clock one morning.

Suddenly things were moving on the Land Army front. Some of the younger men had left the farms, a great deal of marginal land had been put under cultivation and pasture land ploughed up and sown with corn. The Land Army was needed at last. Moreover, farmers had seen that girls could do many jobs as well – and a few even better – than a man. Members now numbered 30,000 but the demand soon outnumbered the supply. Colourful posters, one painted especially for the WLA by an eminent artist, depicted girls among the standing corn, others tractor ploughing.

Most of the girls came from towns: typists, hairdressers, shop assistants with little or no experience of country life, even a few ballet dancers and musicians. Some girls came from the Dominions.

The first week in June, Mrs Jenkins called with my uniform (for which I surrendered most of my clothing coupons) and the good news that I was to report at a small farm at Sway, on the outskirts of the New Forest, the following Monday. My wage would be the regulation 27 shillings and sixpence per week, for which amount the farmer would be reimbursed by the government during my four weeks' training. From this munificent sum fivepence would be deducted for an agricultural insurance stamp and 18 shillings for board and lodging. Most girls were trained on farms, others in training centres or farm institutes, while the Henry Ford Institute of Agricultural Engineering at Boreham ran tractor-driving courses for Land Girls.

There was one last hitch to my getting on the land. No-one in the vicinity of the farm was prepared to billet a Land Girl. Finding suitable billets for her girls was often one of the representative's problems. Girls were billeted in the farmhouses, in cottages where living conditions could be primitive, or in hostels. These ranged from converted henhouses and disused railway carriages to mansions and even castles and were run by the WLA, YWCA and a few by the War Agricultural Committee. Potential landladies in the villages were sometimes loath to take in girls who would need early breakfasts and packed lunches, had large appetites and would perhaps bring mud and straw and hayseeds into the house: sometimes they already had evacuees or billeted soldiers.

My problem was solved by Mrs Jenkins's suggestion that, as Sway was only a few miles from New Milton, I should live at home and commute by bicycle.

On the evening of the 8th June 1940, I laid out my new uniform on my bed and considered it with pride; one pair corduroy breeches, two pairs cotton dungarees, three cotton shirts, a green woollen Jersey, three pairs woollen socks, khaki milking coat, mac, stout shoes, gum boots, hat and tie. To these items I added a stout leather belt, made to measure by the local saddler for half-a-crown.

I laid out the articles I needed for the morning and went to bed early in anticipation of my first day's farm work on the morrow.

The lark that had risen from knee high barley was now invisible, just a paean of song from the cloudless blue sky as I cycled along a blossom-scented lane at 6.30 the next morning. My spirits soared like the lark with the sense of freedom and adventure.

I met other early risers: a milkman, the postman, a man leading two goats, all soon to become familiar figures with whom I exchanged a morning salute. At last I came to a turning and looked for a signpost, momentarily forgetting that, as a wartime precaution they had all been removed. Was this the road I should take?

On the corner an old man was leaning on his garden gate enjoying a first pipe of the day while admiring his neat row of cabbages. He removed the pipe and straightened his back when I asked him the way.

"Tower Farm?"

"Next left, down t'ill, fust farm on left."

He scrutinized me from my brand new hat to my spotless shoes with his keen blue eyes.

"So ee's t'noo land gel."

I nodded.

"Wot's a pretty li'l thing like you want wi' farm work? Still I'm glad you ain't one of they made up, fency bits o' stuff".

Having won that much approval I cycled on, amused by the old man's remarks, although I considered myself to be of sterner stuff than a mere 'pretty little thing'.

I arrived at the farm to witness a rare commotion. The farmer, a retired army major, had been enjoying a little sport, shooting rats in the yard with a rifle, until a bullet had ricocheted off a stone, penetrating the second cowman's gumboot. When he ceased his hopping gyrations about the yard so that the wound could be examined, it turned out to be only a graze. Composure restored, the Major introduced me. The injured man was George. There was Bill, the head cowman, while Sid, the tractor driver, completed the farm staff. I was left in the care of Bill.

"Your first job in the morning", he told me, "is to feed the hens and collect the eggs. You'll find a hand bowl and a sack of wheat in the barn. Then you can help me in the dairy."

About twenty Rhode Island Reds roamed and scratched at will in the yard and adjacent paddock and laid their eggs in a hen house by the barn. There is something delectable about picking a warm, glossy egg from a nest of crisp, sweet hay. It seems quite unrelated to the cold, impersonal objects displayed on trays in shops. In the same way, fragrant milk, straight from the cow, is a very different commodity from the white sterile content of a milk bottle.

I took the eggs to the house, then, wearing a stiff, rubber, armpit to ankle enveloping apron – in which I resembled a length of drain piping – I helped Bill wash the milking utensils, while George turned out the herd of twenty Guernseys and brushed down the cowshed.

I had rinsed the last pail and put it on the rack to drain and was getting out of my straitjacket, when George appeared at the dairy door, still limping slightly.

"Got your hoe?" he enquired.

He fetched one for me from the stable and sharpened it with a file; it was a tool with which I was to become very familiar in the next few weeks. At the gate of the kale field we met the Major again.

"Coming along nicely," he remarked, nodding toward what looked to me like rows of green weeds. "Could do with a good rain though…"

"Aah, a nice rain now before we starts cutting the hay wouldn't hurt at all." Bill agreed.

George had already been over the field with the horse hoe, cutting out the weeds between the rows. Now came the more intricate task of cutting the mass of chickweed, groundsel and dungweed from the tender, blueish plants of kale. Bill, George and Sid made it look easy, but my efforts were slow and uncertain. However, the Major seemed satisfied that I had got the idea.

"Have you got a good back?" he asked with a smile.

"Ask me later" I replied.

"Now I want you to take your hoe and work from the far hedge" he said, indicating the distant side of the field. I looked in some surprise. True, it was years before unisex and Womens' Lib, but I was not prepared for such complete segregation of the sexes. Throughout the long hours while the men worked in a companionable bunch on one side of the field, I made my lone way up and down the interminable rows on the other. Twice daily they hailed me across the empty acres: at midday and milking time.

The Major kindly suggested that I ate my sandwiches in the summerhouse on his lawn, so I passed the dinner hour in the same splendid isolation. It was pleasant though, under the shade of a huge walnut tree, looking onto the multicoloured herbaceous border.

When Bill went down to the meadows to fetch the cows, I helped George to fetch the buckets from the dairy and prepare for the afternoon milking. I awaited the herd as they ambled up from the pasture with growing apprehension. In spite of my determination and my maternal grandmother, I was terrified of cows. Now they came surging through the yard gateway and into the cowpen. There was a rattle of chains as George tied them up in the stalls, a daunting row, their tails swishing angrily at flies. Bill dumped a bucket of hot water in front of me, handed me a cloth and told me I could "get on and wash their udders." Was there a grin on his face as he turned away? Gingerly I approached the first cow and applied the wet cloth to her udder using that swift economy of movement with which a schoolboy washes behind his ears. Bill was grinning openly now.

"You'll have to do a bit more than that," he said. Bravely I 'did a bit more' and finding that the cows made no movement I took heart and finished the row in positively nonchalant style. Then came the actual milking. A placid, easy cow was chosen for me and I took up my little three legged stool. As with other first-time milkers, my inept tugging and squeezing produced only the occasional weak squirt of milk, some of which missed the bucket altogether. From behind me came a sharp 'Ping-Ping' followed by the roar of milk pouring into a bucket from between Bill's expert fingers. After he had taken his full frothing pail to the cooler I followed with mine, containing a few inches of milk with no head at all.

Improvement was slow, but by the end of the week I had graduated to three cows per milking and if I could not raise froth there was at least a rim of bubbles round my pail.

Every morning the kale field waited. Soon I began to enjoy hoeing, seeing the clean, upstanding rows of kale while the weeds, left on top of the ground, withered in the sun.

When we had finished the kale we started on the mangolds. Here the tiny plants had to be singled out as the weeds were cut from them, making the work, for me, slower and more painstaking. The men, with astonishing speed and dexterity, pulled and pushed their hoes as they walked sideways along the line, leaving, with one deft stroke, a single clean mangold plant standing a hoe's breadth from the next.

Still working in solitude on the opposite side of the field I was glad to reach the end of the row and stretch my back.

Looking up, I often witnessed the aerial combat of Spitfires and Messerschmidts, for the Battle of Britain was well under way. Their dark shapes manoeuvred against a blue sky traced with their white vapour trails and dotted with cotton wool puffs of smoke from their machine guns. I heard the accompanying "pop, pop, pop" of gunfire and sometimes the ominous thud of shrapnel falling uncomfortably close. Twice, I watched a plane spiralling downward, one of 'theirs' and one of 'ours', the pilots drifting down after their aircraft under gleaming white parachutes.

In time the overhead 'dogfights' became part of the daily routine and we accepted the falling shrapnel as an occupational hazard. I heard that in the Portsmouth area, girls were issued with tin hats. But our danger was minimal compared with that encountered by girls on the East coast, who worked under constant air attack, and in East Kent under shelling from enemy batteries across the Channel. Some girls had to take cover beneath their tractors when they became targets for German pilot's machine guns. Many girls received bravery awards, not only for carrying on their work under aerial activity but for rescuing cattle from burning buildings, helping to put out ricks set alight by incendiary bombs and, on one occasion, a goods train, and for pulling pilots from burning planes.

In Sussex, a Land Girl narrowly escaped being machine gunned when an enemy plane dived and strafed the road as she cycled to work. Later the same girl was terrified when a Heinkel was shot down overhead while she worked outside a cowshed. As she took shelter in the flimsy building, pieces of metal from the plane clattered onto the roof and larger pieces dropped outside "clanking horribly". Later she went with the farmer and a horse and cart picking up pieces of the plane. The two airmen who parachuted from the plane, were afterwards captured.

The Battle of Britain is remembered by different people in connection with different circumstances, but for many Land Girls it will be bound up with hot summer days and blue skies, with the scent of hay and the green rows of kale.

Blue skies and bright sunlight might be good for spotting enemy planes and for hoeing, but the prolonged hot spell was bad for the grass and consequently for the milk yield.

"Fair breaks yer heart to look in the churn," said Bill.

I began to appreciate the all-importance of weather to the farmer. What to the townsman was another beautiful day, to the grower of crops was another twelve hours without essential rain on his fields.

Every day the sun beat down on our bent backs as we worked.

"'Tis a sight too 'ot" George declared.

I had long since exchanged breeches and jersey for cotton shirt and dungarees, but I noticed that whatever the temperature, the men did not discard their waistcoats or undo a button of their collarless shirts. They never exposed more than their faces and forearms to the elements, "fer fear t' sun do ketch 'old of I," as one old labourer put it. "T' more ee do take off, t' 'otter ee do get," he maintained, believing that plenty of clothing insulated him against the heat.

One morning Sid left us to cut the hay. We could watch the progress of his tractor and mower as it lumbered to and fro across the sloping field, leaving swathes strung across the shorn ground like a shawl draped round the shoulder of the hill, the blades drawing out the essence of the grass and clover until the sweet odours wafted across to us as we worked.

Perhaps the fact that there was hay on the ground changed the weather, for the next morning Bill glanced at the sky as we walked slowly to the mangold field, for even at that hour the heat was oppressive and predicted that a storm was brewing. Sure enough, by mid-morning the sun had gone and when we returned to the field after dinner, pigeon-blue storm clouds were banked over the woods. There was a pregnant stillness in the air, not a leaf stirred and the cows were grouped together under the trees, their tails gyrating at the tormenting flies. Across the field, the men were leaning on their hoes gazing at the sky. A lurid yellow light lay over the swathes of hay transforming them into saffron ribbons.

I went on hoeing in a desultory fashion listening for the first rumble of thunder. When it came it was sudden; a crash overhead, almost simultaneously with a vivid flash of forked lightning. Great spots of rain fell, sizzling on the hot ground.

"Come on!" the men yelled. I needed no second warning and ran after them across field and pasture to the shelter of the buildings.

The storm raged throughout the afternoon but by the end of milking had subsided into muttered rumblings and distant flashes of lightning. The deluge through which we had dashed from cowpen to dairy with buckets of milk, had ceased, leaving that mouldy-sweet smell of rain on parched soil. Several cool, moist days followed.

"I 'low the grass looks greener already," declared Bill, looking out from the cowpen where he and George were lime washing the walls.

My wet weather job was mending hessian sacks. Enthroned on a pile of them, in my usual solitude in the barn, I plied a long, flat, curved needle threaded with string. The next day, while the men mucked out the calf pens, I cut nettles in the yard. George sharpened the rip hook for me with a whetstone.

"Now if you do this," he cautioned me, "keep the sharp side of the blade away from you, mind, and use downward strokes with the stone. You'll cut yourself else".

He showed me how to hold the hook low and level with the ground, cutting the weeds at the base.

Then fine weather returned. The hay dried and was turned. Soon it was ready for carting. For one glorious afternoon I pitched hay into a wagon. This was the life! This was farm work as my grandmother must have enjoyed it! But the next day, while the men went on with the haymaking, I was sent to finish the mangolds. The reason, I could only assume, as I thought I'd done rather well with the pitching, was the Major's reluctance to let me join the men, although a kinder, pleasanter trio I have yet to meet. Up to a point I appreciated his chivalrous care of me, but I did think he was taking it too far and I began to wonder who he was protecting from whom?

The four weeks sped by. With my so-called training at an end I had learned to milk a cow, to handle a hoe and a rip hook and, very briefly, a pitchfork. I had become accustomed to long hours of manual work – there were calluses now where blisters had been. A brunette, I tanned easily and had changed colour in the first week; I even had the beginnings of muscles.

I was ready for my next job.

Bikes and hens, Summer 1941.

CHAPTER 2

To the New Forest

Mr Lush did not really want to employ a Land Girl, but when his second cowman developed an acute appendicitis and was likely to be away for four weeks, he had no alternative.

So on the second Sunday in July, I was driven by car, my bicycle tied to the boot, by another Land Army representative, across the New Forest to Fawley, where my new employer farmed 250 acres.

"It was very good of you to bring me," I said, as she left me at the farmhouse.

"Oh, it's nice to have an excuse to use some petrol and have a little trip. We have enjoyed it," she added, indicating the friend who had accompanied her. "Hope you get on all right".

Mr Lush was an energetic little man who wore a long black moustache and a perpetually anxious expression. His wife, by contrast, resembled the Happy Families picture of the Farmer's Wife, broad of hip and bosom, with rosy cheeks and ample brown hair knotted loosely in a bun. She was strong, cheerful and hardworking.

After giving me tea, she took me round to my billet in a tiny cottage, half a mile from the farm, with a pleasant if somewhat lackadaisical Irish woman whose husband was serving with the Forces.

"You'll be needing to get up early in the morning for the milking," she said when I went to bed the first night. "Will you be needing a call? I sleep late meself".

"That's all right Mrs. Murphy," I replied, "I have an alarm clock." I set the clock for 4.45 but I was already awake when the first yellow-grey light dispelled the darkness of my room.

I got up and let myself out of the back door without disturbing Mrs Murphy. As I took my bicycle out of the shed the crimson rim of the sun rose above Southampton Water. This was the first time in my life that I had been out before dawn. As I cycled to the farm with the sunrise casting a magical glow over the fields, sniffed the cool air, pure as spring water, I regretted all the mornings of my life that I had been between blankets at that hour.

When I reached the farm, the herd of Dairy Shorthorns was ambling up from the meadows, looming out of a layer of mist, the slanting rays of the sun enhancing their colours of red and strawberry roan.

The wonder of this early morning when I was just eighteen, called to mind the lines of Wordsworth,

'Bliss was it that dawn to be alive, But to be young was very heaven.'

After we had tied them up in the stalls, warm and steaming and smelling of the grass and the mist, Mr Lush and the head cowman put on the machines while Mrs Lush and I stripped out the milk that remained in the udder after they were removed. I thought stripping was tedious work and much preferred milking entirely by hand.

"Now what can I give you to do?" asked Mr Lush after breakfast, pushing back his hat, scratching his head and looking at me with his worried gaze.

"I can hoe." I said, seeing the men on their way to the mangold field.

"Never did know a woman make a good job of hoeing", he replied.

Proud of my new found skill I took umbrage at this. In the end I was turned out by myself in a large meadow to pull ragwort, that ubiquitous yellow weed that must, by law, be removed from pasture.

"Every bit must be picked up an' taken from the field," said the old labourer who found me a wheelbarrow for the purpose. "Fer ef t' cows do eat et when et do git droi, et do poisin they."

In spite of their flamboyant heads the plants had little root and it was not a hard task to pull them and cart them away. I enjoyed those hours in the field in the fresh air and the hot sun. It is not possible to describe the happiness, almost exhilaration, shared by so many other girls in those early days on the land. Perhaps it was from an innate desire, not even realised but now fulfilled, to escape from the claustrophobic life of the town into the freedom and freshness of the countryside.

I was not so euphoric about the hour between the midday meal and the afternoon milking when I washed milk bottles from the round which Mr Lush did with the big, old farm car. Wrapped in the inevitable long, rubber apron and a cloud of steam, I scrubbed them with a long handled brush, then rinsed them in the other half of the double galvanised sink. When I had filled them with the afternoon's milk and put them into crates for the morning delivery it was time to go home. I felt by then that I would like to get into a hot bath myself, but when I asked Mrs Murphy that evening if I might have one, she looked at me in pained surprise.

"Indaid you can't," she replied with some asperity. "Tis Fridays I light the copper for baths!"

After five days of washing piecemeal in cold water in a small hand basin on the washstand in my bedroom, I welcomed Friday like the first day of spring!

"I suppose you'll be wanting your bath," said Mrs. Murphy grudgingly that evening. "You'll find it hanging on the wall by the back door."

It was the smallest zinc bath I had ever seen; I used a bigger one at home for bathing my dog.

"Is this it?" I asked.

"It is indaid," answered my landlady briskly, as if wondering what more I could be wanting.

I carried the inadequate little tub up to my room and fetched two buckets of water from the copper. Remembering Archimedes principle I thought that was all it would contain beside my person. By adopting the foetal position I managed to sit down, not realising my mistake until I tried to get up. I was wedged as tightly as a cork in a bottle. Wriggling, and rocking to and fro only resulted in near capsize. I sat in the fast-cooling water and contemplated my situation. Perhaps I could crawl downstairs, bath on back, tortoise fashion, to enlist Mrs Murphy's help. I even envisaged the local fire brigade arriving with a metal cutting device. My anxiety was in no way relieved by the sudden banshee wailing of the air raid siren.

"I'm going down to the shelter!" Mrs Murphy called up the stairs. "You'd best come too."

But I was in no position to go anywhere. Perhaps I should go wearing my tin bath? Maybe if I just rolled over it would serve as a mini-shelter. It occurred to me that a good bomb blast might solve my predicament!

Very soon came the sound of enemy bombers flying in over Southampton Water, the heavy throb of their engines finding an echo in the beating of my heart; then a deafening barrage from the anti-aircraft guns posted nearby, made the walls of the old cottage tremble. Stuck in my bath I felt utterly alone and scared. Five, ten minutes passed, while the planes droned overhead amid a crescendo of engine noise and gunfire. At the height of the cacophony there was a vivid flare of light followed by a tremendous explosion. The floor rocked and I freed my left leg.

As I was dressing the 'all clear' sounded.

"There was an enemy plane shot down over Calshot last night" Mrs Lush told me the next morning. "Did you hear it?"

I told her just where I was when I heard it.

"Oh, my dear," she laughed, "You can have baths here whenever you like. There is always plenty of hot water."

Afterwards, whenever I was billeted in a cottage without 'mod cons', anyone who invited me in for a bath where hot water came out of a tap and disappeared down a plughole was my friend for life!

The problem of the bath resolved, there was still that 'last thing before retiring' walk to the bottom of the garden.

I was not yet sufficiently a country girl to ignore the bats, night flying insects, strange noises and dark shadows I encountered on the long overgrown path, or to remain indifferent to the creepy crawlies I could not see. They lurked in the wood crevices and the ivy that encroached inside, as well as over, that primitive little loo.

My return was a headlong scramble to the back door. To think that I had once taken indoor sanitation for granted! I imagined these conditions in the dark nights and early mornings of winter, with the rain or icy winds penetrating the gaps in the dilapidated hut. But winter was a long way off and by the time it arrived I hoped I would be in more salubrious lodgings.

My mornings were still occupied with field weeding. When the ragwort was cleared there were other weeds to be dealt with; the tall spear thistles and the fragrant but invasive creeping thistle. I slew them all with a heavy, pick-axe like tool called a mattock. Their downy seed heads floated gently on the light breeze; a charm of goldfinches fed on the few plants I had purposely left for them in the hedge. Always content with my own company I enjoyed the solitude of the meadows; it heightened my observation of all that moved: a kestrel quartering the field; brimstone butterflies feeding on scabious and knapweed. One day I watched two kestrels fighting fiercely with beak and claw until one backed down and flew away.

There were deadlier combats too, in the sky, for here, near Calshot, I again witnessed the fighting of allied and enemy planes. From the field I could see the two great barrage balloons, gleaming silver, 5,000 feet up over Southampton. In the evening I could watch them travelling up the water, mounted on the decks of vessels, to Calshot Point where they were moored for the night, giving some protection from enemy aircraft.

1940 was the only consistently hot summer of the war. The temperature stayed in the upper 70's for weeks on end. I could stand the heat in the open field but afternoon milking was sheer misery: the humidity of the cowpen, sitting clammy with sweat close to a restless cow, the pain as the end of her tail flicked my eye, stinging bites from the vicious New Forest fly which were tormenting her too. Milking in summer was for the cool of the early morning. My least popular job was removing warble fly maggots from the cows' backs. At this time of the year the cattle were attacked by warble flies which laid their eggs under the skin. These hatched into maggots and when we saw the ominous lump they made, the only remedy was to squeeze them out with the fingers: a revolting process.

On weekdays I had my midday meals at the farmhouse, for which I was grateful; the height of Mrs Murphy's culinary efforts was a watery vegetable soup, unflavoured with salt, which she maintained was 'bad for you'.

Mrs Lush's cooking, like everything else that she did, was excellent. I was surprised to see on the table with a substantial hot meal, a quart jug of milk from which Mr Lush drank several glasses.

I worked from 5am to 5pm, but my evenings were free. Many of them were taken up with learning to ride. A hundred yards or so down the lane from my billet, where it petered out into marshland and Ashlett Creek, was a tall regency house with adjacent yard, stables and barn. Here the daughter of the house kept a few forest ponies and gave riding lessons at 2/6d an hour. My spending money sometimes ran to three lessons a week. My first mount was a placid mare named Molly. On her back, following the white pony tracks across the heath or the leaf-strewn paths through the oak woods, began for me an enchantment with the New Forest that has remained to this day. Felicity, my instructress, was a plump, pretty girl of seventeen, with an upturned nose, generously freckled, brown curly hair and laughing green eyes. Like most of the young people in the vicinity she had ridden for as long as she had walked and was equally at home on horseback with or without a saddle. She could mount like an Indian, either by holding the pony's mane and leaping on from the side, or running up behind and leap-frogging into the saddle. To me, at a time when mounting was still a carefully considered operation, this seemed a quite remarkable feat. She rode a small wild black pony by the name of Black Jack, which only she could control. He would, when she whispered in his ear, buck into a near vertical position and spin round on his front legs. No-one but Felicity whispered in his ear. Many evenings when we had Black Jack and Molly saddled up the air raid siren would sound across the fields from Calshot and we had to put them back in the stable and wait for the 'All Clear'.

"Mother doesn't like us to be riding during an alert," said Felicity. "We used to have wonderful moonlight rides before the war spoilt things. We would start off when the moon was rising and take food, a kettle and frying pan on a pack pony and have a picnic somewhere in the forest".

I spent most of my free time at Ashlett. That the house was horse orientated was apparent as one entered the front door. There was always a saddle on the newel post, a bridle hanging on a door. There might be a pony in the hall in search of a tit-bit. Other saddles, bridles or halters were encountered on the way through the kitchen to the stable yard. Ethel, who was cook, housekeeper and general factotum, tried ineffectually to bring some order to the household but was frequently called from the task to bandage a pony's tail, hold a yearling while Felicity branded it with an iron heated on the kitchen stove, or help blister a leg, all of which she did with long suffering cheerfulness.

Felicity constantly gathered round her a group of teenage riders, mostly the sons and daughters of local farmers or tradespeople, all of whom rode forest ponies, some reared and broken by themselves. The very best mount for riding in the forest, especially for the young or inexperienced, is the native pony, for he knows the tracks and the bogs, and if his rider is lost can usually find the way home. He is sure footed over the rough heath; he will scramble down the ragged, precipitous slopes and across the rocky bottom of a stream and happily ford the deep pools that are a feature of some parts of the forest. All this I did on Molly during the early days of my riding, for as soon as I was off the leading rein I rode with Felicity's 'gang'. They numbered about six to eight although the only one that I can remember now is Eric, a fair, fresh complexioned pleasant boy, the son of Fawley's butcher. As they had all ridden since they were toddlers and I was still a learner, following their fast and reckless progress over all obstacles (there was no way I could stop Molly doing what the other ponies did) resulted in my hitting the ground hard and often. They say that it takes seven falls to make a rider. In this respect I qualified very quickly.

Molly had one very annoying habit. She was a 'jibber'. Most ponies will keep going in the company of others, but Molly would decide that she had had enough, even when her companions were in full gallop across a heath. No effort of mine would budge her and there I had to sit until one of the others, usually Eric, turned to see a diminishing figure in the far distance and rode back to my rescue.

Meanwhile my work at the farm had settled down to a steady routine of milking, field weeding, bottle-washing and milk bottling. Sometimes I helped Mr Lush's twenty-year old daughter, Dorothy, who was a herbalist, to weed and hoe in her herb garden, or dug potatoes with Mrs Lush for the house. Four weeks passed swiftly. The second cowman's convalescence was over and Mr Lush needed me no more. Neither, it seemed, did anyone else.

My local WLA representative was now a Mrs Brown.

"I do hope we can find a job for you," she said when she called on me one morning a few days before I was due to leave. I hoped so too. It would be an anti-climax to return home and wait yet again, and I was loath to leave the Forest, the riding, and my new-found friends.

It was Eric who found the solution to my problem. The retail dairyman at Blackfield, a neighbouring village, needed a girl to help with his milk round, he told me.

"It isn't exactly landwork, but you could perhaps do it far a while," he said.

I went to see Mr Soffe, a six-foot-four farmer's son, with a red, jovial face and bright ginger hair. When I said that I would like to come and work for him his only question was, "When can you start?"

Mrs Brown said that if he applied for a Land Girl in the usual way she would arrange for me to take the job. She also found me a billet with a young couple in a modern house in Blackfield village.

I started work the following Monday.

CHAPTER 3

The Milk Round

It was a funny little handcart, like a large orange box painted bright green on two pneumatic tyres, with a sort of pram handle in front. Mr Soffe was loading it with crates of milk when I arrived at the dairy at 6.30am.

"I want you to deliver to the nearby cottages with this," he explained. "There are thirty of them. I'll come with you this morning and show you."

We crossed the road and turned left by the butcher's shop. I pushed the cart which was well balanced and ran easily. In a long narrow lane with cottages on either side were my first customers. I probably saw them at that early hour as few others did. Men unshaven, women with hair uncombed or in rollers, half naked babies crawling on the floor.

The tarmac gave way to rough gravel as we came to a circle of scattered dwellings on the edge of the common. The fronts looked out onto a wide expanse of short turf where pigs roamed with a flock of geese and a few cows, those attractive brindles which I have only seen in the New Forest. The colour is achieved, I was told, by crossing Guernsey with Dairy Shorthorn.

I was wary of the gander which came at me, scolding harshly with craned neck and outstretched wings, and I brandished a milk bottle as a weapon of defence in case his display was not all empty threat. I was leaning into the cart to reach a bottle for the last house when a voice behind me asked: "'ave ee got a hextry 'alf pint sonny?" I turned to see an old forester from one of the cottages. "Oh, sorry Miss, I thought ee were a lad!"

"The locals aren't used to girls doing mens' jobs yet," laughed Mr Soffe when I told him. I would have thought, though, that a pair of Land Army breeches from behind were unmistakable.

The second morning I accomplished my early round alone while Mr Soffe loaded up the van for the main round. This covered a radius of some twenty miles, sometimes in built-up areas, sometimes on the borders of the Forest. I enjoyed getting to know the customers. Soon I was sharing their pleasure and excitement when a husband or son was coming home on leave, or their anxiety when a letter was overdue. Relief was mine, too, a few days later when I was met by a smiling face.

"You have heard from your son, Mrs Jones?"

"Oh yes, yes my dear – and he's all right".

Then there was that form for a free pint of milk that divulged to the milk-girl a secret long before the neighbours knew. They in turn showed a kindly concern for me. That I would "catch my death" from getting wet through. On seeing me still hale and hearty next day they remarked in almost offended surprise, "None the worse for your wetting, then?"

I became on waving terms with many people whom I never spoke to but saw regularly in the same place each day; a postman and a baker on their rounds; the driver of a milk lorry collecting churns from a stand by a farm gate; a herdsman turning out the cows; so many in fact that at times my hand was perpetually raised like the Queen's on a royal tour.

I got to know the dogs, too: large ones with wet tongues and ecstatic welcomes; suspicious ones that saw me off the premises with a baleful glance and throaty growl; indifferent ones that lay by the door and merely opened an eye at my approach.

A familiar figure on my round was Fawley's popular local doctor, Eric Jones-Evans, a big, handsome man, who, wearing a broad brimmed hat and often a wide shouldered cloak, went his rounds on horseback.

Of brilliant versatility, he was a qualified surgeon, while his somewhat larger than life personality reflected his great love – the theatre. He achieved local fame as an actor, singer, producer, writer and theatrical historian.

The afternoons were perhaps the most enjoyable part of the day, for when I had done up my account book and helped Mr Soffe with the bottle washing we did another round, this time collecting milk from several farms. This took us along winding leafy lanes, past the wild and lovely saltings at Lepe, and through beautiful parkland to the Rothchild dairy at Beaulieu. This dairy and cow pens were equipped in what was, for those days, the height of hygienic modernity, with high white tiled walls, wide aisles, steel tubular fittings and automatic drinking bowls. Two very pretty and efficient Land Girls coped with the herd of pedigree Shorthorns.

On the third afternoon Mr Soffe stopped the van in a quiet lane and got out.

"Move over," he said, "I'm going to teach you to drive. Then you can do the round yourself sometimes and give me a day off."

I moved over apprehensively; always happier with things on four legs than on wheels I was not keen on the idea of driving. Besides, kind and good natured as Mr Soffe usually was, I had already found him to have an explosive temper – and he was very proud of his new Austin 10 van.

The start was not too promising. The fact that the van had a very fierce clutch did not help. I first stalled the engine, then started off with many jerks and jumps. Mr Soffe's patience was wearing thin when the vehicle finally leapt forward and kept going.

After that I got on pretty well, I thought, and even my instructor had begun to relax when I took a bend a little too fast and found myself on a collision course with a road sign.

"Put your foot down!" yelled Mr Soffe, in a voice that drove all coherent thought from my mind. I put my foot down – hard. It was a pity it was still on the accelerator. The resulting impact did the van's right-hand wing no good at all.

Mr Soffe controlled himself magnificently, but I was concerned about the colour of his face.

He took over then while he recovered his nerve, but when we came to the Rothchild farm he drove into a field and we changed places again. For half-an-hour I practised driving and reversing between cow pats; using them as imaginary gateposts.

The driving lessons continued daily. I learned to reverse round the corners of farm buildings and through narrow gateways when collecting the milk, until there was only one thing left to master. Between the dairy and the road was a long, narrow driveway hemmed in by high hedges. Although I could now back at almost any angle I could not back straight.

I made repeated attempts, while Mr Soffe danced up and down at the dairy door shouting and gesticulating, his face that extraordinary hue that made me fear for his blood pressure. The whole operation was extremely wearing on his temper and my nerves, to say nothing of the hedge. But at last I managed to keep to the straight and narrow way and so onto the road.

The next day Mr Soffe left me to drive round the farms by myself while he went to a funeral. I reversed faultlessly out of the drive but I should not have let success make me reckless. For safety, I should have allowed far more room to turn by the deep ditch outside the gate, but I took a risk. It was one of the rare days that summer when rain had made the verge soft and slippery. My offside wheels skidded as they touched it, and the van slid slowly but inevitably into the ditch.

It was still there when Mr Soffe returned from the funeral. I clearly remember a six foot four embodiment of fury as, with shaking fists high above his head, he left his two surprised and dismayed companions, and bore down upon me.

An hour later we set off on the round together in strained silence, but typically, by the time we reached home he was himself again, and by the next day appeared to have forgotten the whole incident and sent me off once more by myself.

As I reached Copse Farm, my first stop, I felt conscious of being on my own and – as is often the case when one is doing a job alone for the first time – the unprecedented and unexpected happened.

The bull, a great red beefy shorthorn, was usually in the yard with the cows. Never before had he been lying just inside the gate, completely blocking the narrow gangway between the barn and the cartshed.

First I tried verbal persuasion, but he ignored my gentle "Come on, boy, get up." Then I tried prodding him with my foot, even a restrained kick, but he seemed not to notice. It was useless to call Sid, the cowman. He would not have heard above the noise of the generator and the milking machine. The only way was to climb over the recumbent beast. Cautiously I slid one leg over his broad back, eyeing his massive neck and stout horns. His girth felt enormous as I straddled it. He did not move, but heaved a deep sigh which elevated my position several inches. Carefully I drew over my other leg, stood up and walked quickly across the yard.

"I had to climb over your bull" I told Sid.

He grinned. "Aah, 'ee don't like movin' don't Albert!" I wondered how we were going to get out with a full ten gallon churn, but when we reached the bull Sid merely shouted.

"Hup there now, Albert!" and Albert 'hupped' slowly and with great effort and ambled away to join his harem. I wondered if I would have to climb over him often. Perhaps next time I would try shouting "Hup there now, Albert".

Heath Farm lay a mile or so down a narrow lane flanked by deep ditches. I was about half way, keeping a careful distance from the verge – I was vary of ditches – when I heard approaching heavy traffic.

"Please, not an army convoy…" I murmured, in a fervent prayer – which was ignored.

Rounding a bend lumbered the first heavy lorry, taking up most of the road. But my guardian angel had not completely deserted me. He suddenly provided a convenient gateway into which I drew my little van. There it cowered while the great green monsters trundled past, each scowling down from its superior height; then followed a dozen flippant little trucks that flapped their canvas roofs mockingly. When at last the lane was quiet, I stole out of my refuge and went on my way.

Mrs Warne, the farmer's wife, was sitting outside the back door of the farmhouse plucking cockerels. She called out to me.

"On your own today?"

I walked across the yard and told her about the hazards I had so far encountered.

"There's bound to be a third," I said. "Things always happen to me in threes. It's become my pet superstition."

She smiled. "Never meet trouble half way. You seem to have got over the others all right."

"I'll probably get a puncture or something out by the saltings where there isn't a soul in sight. I'd rather sit here and help you pluck birds," I said, watching the brown feathers lifted by a sudden breeze. "Don't I wish you could; I've ten to do. There's no end to work these days! And I've all the farm accounts to do. There's so much paperwork these days what with forms and permits and suchlike. Jim has a job to keep up with the farm work, too. He's just getting in the second hay crop and the oats are ready to cut – and taters to get up".

I could see some pastures full of thistles and ragwort too. He wanted a good Land Girl, I thought. I said so to Mr Soffe on the round next day, with the result that I was lent to Mr Warne for one day to clean his fields.

When I'd finished my early round I cycled to Heath Farm, a packet of Spam sandwiches and a bottle of lemonade for my lunch in my saddlebag. The farm seemed deserted. Mr and Mrs Warne had gone to market. I was glad that they managed to get off the place sometimes. There was a wheelbarrow and a mattock left for me by the field gate.

The morning was hot and still. Nothing stirred but a bunch of heifers grazing near the wood on the far side of the next field. I put my lunch and jacket down by the fence and started work.

It was a long way to the end of the field and back again, making frequent trips to the yard to empty the barrow of ragwort. I noticed that the heifers had moved over to the fence. They had obviously spotted me with the barrow, and, inquisitive girls that they were, had come to see what was happening. One was giving my jacket a good going over, and another was waving an empty paper bag in its mouth. An empty paper bag? Where was my lunch? When I reached the fence six heifers retreated slowly, six broad faces gazed at me in wide eyed innocence. One had just finished devouring the paper bag and seemed to find it very tasty. There was not a crumb of my sandwiches to be seen. Although they had rolled the bottle round a bit my drink was still intact, but it was a long hungry day.

"Aah, heifers will eat anything", said Mr Soffe next day. "You have to be careful what you leave around".

Most of my spare time and money was still spent on riding. Now that I had weekend afternoons off, I could go with Felicity & Co on their long forest rides. Some evenings I hired a pony from the local butcher. Seldom indoors, when not on horseback I cycled or walked, alone or with Felicity, who now had an Old English Sheepdog pup requiring a lot of exercise. But that long, hot summer of 1940 finally came to an end. There was a nip in the air as I set out on my early round and layers of mist floated above the heath like strands of white chiffon. The tawny hues of the oaks matched the withering fronds of the bracken, and the ponies grew their winter coats. Another month and they gathered near human habitation, rime on their backs and shrouded by the steam of their breath.

It was dark on the first round and when I called at Heath Farm at the end of the day, the Warnes were milking by the light of hurricane lanterns. I spent my evenings indoors now, sitting with Mr & Mrs Reece, listening to the radio and knitting khaki balaclava helmets or sailors' sea boot stockings from thick, white, oiled wool, or, all too often mending my own land army socks, which were not up to the many hours of walking in gumboots or heavy regulation shoes. Each day on the round produced a fresh crop of holes, and as headquarters were reluctant to issue new socks while anything of the original feet remained, I nightly darned new darns over old darns.

As the nights grew longer so did the air raids, and more intense. The local target was the nearby oil refinery at Fawley, but we could also hear the bombs on Southampton. Then an AA gun was posted in a field at the end of the road and nightly windows were shaken and our ears were deafened by its fire.

The Reeces spent night after night in the air raid shelter along with the neighbours. At first they were very distressed that I would not join them. "We can't leave you in the house alone" they said. But having spent part of a night in a shelter and worked through the next day in a state of somnambulation I decided to take my chances in bed!

The oil refinery, or 'AGWI' as we knew it then, was never bombed, but Fawley's fine Norman Church had a direct hit, so did the house two doors from my billet. A little of the ceiling came down on my bed that night and I thought perhaps I should go downstairs and pass the rest of the night on the sofa. But it must have been just jettisoned bombs, for everything quietened down after that. I shook the plaster out of my bedclothes and went back to sleep.

There were a few bright spots of entertainment in that long, dull winter. In November I went to a dance at Beaulieu Abbey with Felicity and her mother and two friends of the family, Robert, a young army subaltern, Keith, a Spitfire pilot and Eric.

I had thought it absurd to pack a long dress among my Land Army togs, but now it came out for an airing. It was layers of pink and mauve net over taffeta and the full skirt felt strange round my legs which for months had been clad in breeches or dungarees. The low neck revealed a V of fading suntan and my nearly developed biceps looked incongruous beneath the tiny puff sleeves.

Felicity and her mother, whom I had never seen in anything else but shirts and jodhpurs, also looked unusually feminine.

"The grubs have become butterflies!" they laughed.

The dance was held in the refectory hall, where great limbs of trees blazed on the long hearth. The heat grew so intense Keith said he felt as if he had been shot down in flames. Outside the night was clear and still. As we drove home, searchlights playing over Southampton were the only activity in the sky.

Another evening when there was a lull in the air raids Felicity and I went to the Picturedrome at Hythe on Southampton Water to see the film *The Mikado*. The cinema was little more than a hut with a corrugated iron roof. Half way through the performance, torrential rain fell and the din on the tin roof completely drowned the music and dialogue for the rest of the film. Shortly before Christmas we went into Southampton to do some seasonal shopping, Felicity driving the family car in the way that she rode horses, with reckless abandon. The result was at times hair-raising.

Although my life and work at Blackfield was pleasant enough, in the New Year I grew restless. I had joined the Land Army to work on a farm and this I still wanted to do. I talked to Mr Soffe about it and he was very understanding. Mrs Brown agreed to arrange a transfer.

My last two weeks on the round were the worst of the winter. No snow fell, but freezing conditions made driving hazardous. There was one day when freezing rain fell and ice covered the roads. Mr Soffe was ill with 'flu and I was on my own. His only advice was "Don't use your brakes or you'll turn right round". It was not reassuring, but I finished the delivery.

When I went to Ashlett to say goodbye, Felicity had volunteered for the FANY's, Eric was about to join the RAF, another member of the gang had been called up for the army. By the spring we would have all gone our separate ways.

Horse and Haycart, 1941.

CHAPTER 4

Trouble with Brownie

A straight but undulating ribbon of road passes through rich beech woods and alternating expanses of turf and heath between Brockenhurst and Lyndhurst.

Lying a little back from the road about a mile from Brockenhurst Bridge are the kennels of the New Forest Buckhounds, and about as far again a second gravel drive branches off from the road, passes through white gates by a white painted lodge and continues between iron fenced farm land to a farmhouse with its surrounding yard and complex of buildings.

Here I arrived one moist Sunday afternoon in February and was greeted by Mr Gough – "the boss" – who took me indoors to meet his wife, his daughter Doris, and Joy, a fellow Land Girl. A handsome Irish Setter called Bray and a number of cats in assorted colours and sizes made up the household.

Over tea the boss explained my job. It was, in part, another milk round, but with a difference. This time the means of transport was a pony and float, of a vintage now only found in Agricultural Museums. Joy did a second round with a similar vehicle. Time not spent on the round would be occupied with general farm work.

After the meal when there was little light left except that provided by the log fire, Mrs Gough lit an oil lamp and placed it in the middle of the table.

"This is only a temporary measure" the boss explained. "We have calor gas lighting but I haven't managed to get the cylinders this week".

Washing up in the kitchen was done by the light of a candle. Hot water for the washing up came from a copper in the washhouse opposite the back door. The copper, heated by a log fire, which permeated the house and buildings with the odour of wood smoke, provided all the hot water for the house and dairy. Taking a bath, as I discovered in due course, entailed pumping up the water by means of a tall hand pump. It was then necessary to dash upstairs and undress quickly before the water cooled.

The family retired early. Doris and Joy, who had been friends long before Joy came to work on the farm, shared a room. I had a large double bed to myself in a room that looked over the yard to a pasture and beech woods beyond.

The boss called me at 6am. This gave me time to get my breakfast and load up the float ready to start the round at 7 o'clock. The kitchen was deserted at that hour except for the cats. Mrs Gough rose in time to cook for the boss and Doris, who worked in an office in Southampton, and Joy who started later on her round. I found bacon in the larder and eggs on the dresser and cooked them over a small oil stove; the big black range was not lit until mid-morning. As I ate I listened to the usual cacophony of morning milking. Men's voices, the clatter of buckets and churns, a distorted rendering of popular music from an old radio strapped to a beam in the cow-pen.

The boss put his head round the back door.

"Forgot to tell you. If you go round to the stable when you've had your breakfast Joe will show you how to harness the pony."

Joe Fripp, from whom I was to take over the round, was a middle aged rotund man with a loud voice that seemed never to be silent. He wore a cloth cap back to front which accentuated the roundness of his pink face and blue eyes, giving him the appearance of a mature baby.

"I'll get Brownie in fer you mornin's, but you'll 'ave t' harness 'er an' get 'er in t' float yersel'" he boomed. "So you wants t' watch 'ow I does it."

I watched carefully as Joe put on first the collar, then the bridle, then on went the pad and breeching. He put the crupper under Brownie's long, full tail, and having backed her into the float, he fastened the breeching.

"Got it?" he boomed. I hoped so.

Back at the dairy we loaded first the big seventeen gallon churn, resplendent with its bands of brass and heavy brass plunger. Joe and I lifted it by stages into the float. First onto the back step, then to the floor of the float, then onto the seat at the front. A ten gallon churn went up next, followed by the crates of bottles and finally the can with its brass handle and hinges and the pint and half pint dippers.

My driving tuition was perfunctory in the extreme.

"'Ere, take yer ribbins," said Joe, handing me the reins as we started off down the drive. I took them and looked over the front rails of the float, along the stout back of Brownie, an aged, bay, forest pony, to her head, which seemed a mile away. I could feel no contact with her mouth. Brownie stopped, then moved slowly on with a zig-zag gait like a stout woman doing a rumba.

"Aah, yer wants t' drop 'er one," said Joe, indicating the whip in its holder. I used it tentatively. Brownie lunged forward for a few yards then went back to her former gradual progress.

"Yer wants t' drop 'er a good un," instructed Joe. "It ain't no good keep ticklin' 'er arse. Give er un 'er'll remember!"

I gave her a smart tap with the whip. Lifting her head she leaned into the bit. We went out of the white gates at speed, the high iron rimmed wheels grating on the drive.

Our first call was the Balmer Lawn Hotel, then an army officers' training college, where I left the ten gallon churn. In the kitchen ATS cooks were already at work, lifting heavy pans on to great hot stoves. Whatever the conditions on my milk round, I thought, I would not change my job for theirs.

Similar to my former round, this one lay partly in areas of close houses extending to the forest fringe, across green lawns and over rough tracks to isolated cottages. Nearing the end of the round we crossed the Weirs, a hilly expanse of heath bordered by a few squatters' cottages. Away from the road, two forestry men were burning the dead bracken and coarse heather; the crackling bright orange flames tapered into billowy acrid smoke which drifted away across the open ground.

"They burns off the bracken and heather in the early spring, so's the noo grass'll come through," Joe explained. "Better grazing fer the ponies and cattle."

We left the isolation of the Weirs for an area of large, well spaced houses, then crossed the water splash into Brocken-hurst's main street. A few calls here and we were on our way home, just stopping at the Balmer Lawn to pick up an empty churn. Brownie was trotting smartly with her head towards home when we came to an opening into the wood. A man was manoeuvring a lorry load .of timber while his mate directed him. Suddenly he held up his hand and shouted "Whoa!" in a voice that rivalled Joe's. Now, one thing I had learned about Brownie, she stopped with alarming suddenness at the mere whisper of that command. Even Joe kept the word reasonably low key. Now she stopped dead, almost sitting down in the shafts. My feet shot from under me and I embraced the churn lid, my nose colliding with the plunger. I looked down at Joe who was draped gracefully across a bottle crate.

"Aah… yer wants t' watch out when anyone shouts 'Whoa'," he said reflectively.

"How did I know he was going to shout 'Whoa'?" I replied, gently fingering my nose. Joe stood up and adjusted his cap which had fallen over one eye.

"Aah, yer wants t' watch out fer little things like that."

I thought it over while we drove back to the farm.

Joy's float, a later model than mine, with small wheels that boasted pneumatic tyres, was already in the shed. Joy had finished her lunch and was washing bottles in the dairy.

After we had unloaded the float Joe rinsed out the churns and bucket while I unharnessed and fed Brownie. By now it was 1.30 and my 6 o'clock breakfast was long forgotten. Mr & Mrs Gough had also had their meal and gone out. The remains of a shepherd's pie, waiting for me in the oven, had not improved with keeping hot, but I attacked it with ravenous appetite.

When we had finished the churns and bottles, few on this round because most of our customers had milk loose from the can, Joy and I went out to cut kale. I liked Joy. She was a happy, good-natured girl, my own age. With her stocky build, straight fair hair and spectacles she was the type who would have captained the hockey team at school. In the eight months I had spent in the Land Army she was the first fellow Land Girl I had met and I enjoyed her company. She had left a job in the civil service early in the war to work on the farm. Used to kale cutting, she found me a bill hook and showed me how to sever the long, thick stems as near as possible to the root and place them in small piles to be loaded onto the cart pulled by an old brown Shire mare.

Slowly leading the mare was a tall, thin, stooping figure in an army greatcoat several sizes too large and a battered trilby. At intervals, between lighting his pipe which seemed to be perpetually going out, he lackadaisically lifted a bunch of kale onto the cart. This was Arthur Witcher, doyen of a family of gypsies who lived in the compound outside the New Park enclosure.

His inability to work at anything approaching a normal speed was attributed by Arthur to a wound received in the First World War. There were certain jobs it prevented him doing altogether.

"Tis me arm, guvner, you know how 'tis with me arm. Can't get et up no 'igher then thet, guvner", he would whine, raising the arm stiffly a few inches from his side. "You know I'd do anythin' fer you, guvner, but 'tis me arm..."

"All right, Arthur," the boss would comply. "Like some tobacco?"

"Aah, thank ee, guvner!" Gleefully he would fill his pipe and light up, striking the match with a flourish that lifted the bad arm to shoulder level.

Many years before, Arthur's wife had walked out on him, leaving him to rear their only son, Johnnie, now a tall, dark-haired youth who would have been handsome but for an unhealthy pallor and an expression which suggested a mentality less than his sixteen years. Arthur did not 'get on' with the rest of the Witcher family, his brother Henry and his wife Harriet, their daughters Connie and Tessa and "'lil 'enry" – undersized but as quick witted as Johnnie was dim. Fierce arguments between the brothers often led to blows, usually over some slight, real or imagined, to 'young Johnnie' or "li'l 'enry".

We went on cutting kale until it was time to start bottling the afternoon's milk. As we walked back across the fields we saw the huntsman in his white coat walking the hounds. We watched their eager waving white sterns disappear among the trees and heard the sharp crack of Jack's whip and his voice calling, "Come-up, Rastus! Come-up Rory! Come-up there my lads! Come-up Rory... RORY, you raking brute!"

From the dairy we heard another voice. Joe Fripp was milking and his chatter reverberated from the far end of the cow pen like a ship's fog horn. He stopped talking only to burst into song, the one item of his repertoire being the first verse of 'Nellie Dean' interspersed with shouts to the cows or remarks to his companions. It went something like this:

"*There's an old mill by the stream* – Get up, Daisy! – *Nellie Dean, Where we used to sit* – Stand still will yer! – *and dream – Nellie Dean. And the waters as they flow* – Jerry dropped a few bombs on Southampton last night, you know – direct hit on a house near the Missus's sister – *used to whisper sweet and low* – Stand still you baggage! – Missus wants 'er t' come an' live along wi' us but she says 'itler ain't drivin' 'er out of 'er "ouse, not while its standing. *You are my heart's desire, I love yer, Nellie Dean.*"

The last rendered with great feeling and libration.

"Makes up in emotion what it lacks in music!" laughed Joy.

By the end of the week I was doing the round by myself and getting to know my new customers. Now it was no longer a matter of leaving a bottle on the doorstep. They chatted while I filled their clean shining jugs from the can. Some were waiting, jug in hand when I walked up the path; others never had one ready.

There was one old lady who must have fed largely on carrots for she brought out a huge bunch of tops each day for Brownie. Another seemed to be always baking, in spite of the rationing, and would put a delicious congress tart or angel cake into my hand.

I remember two elderly horsewomen I met daily; one who was always riding on the Weirs. Impeccably dressed in black habit and hunting bowler she rode side saddle a flighty black mare which persistently cantered sideways, moving lightly across the heath like black thistledown. Near Balmer Lawn Green a heavily-built lady rode an equally sturdy chestnut horse. She wore breeches and boots, tweed jacket and felt hat and rode astride.

We were joined most evenings by the crew of the RAF beacon which stood in the corner of the farmyard, in appearance rather like a Dalek, with a flashing light at the head. With others across the countryside it indicated a flight path for our bomber and fighter planes or possibly an escape route for planes unable to reach their base. It was manned by an RAF Corporal, Vince, and two Aircraftsmen, Bob and

Philip, who were billeted at a nearby smallholding but preferred our fireside. Vince, a short, stocky, dark-haired man we called "the little Corporal". Phil and Bob were boyish and light-hearted and their easy banter enlivened our evenings while the strong, eerie light of the beacon, shining through the landing, window, illumined our way to bed and the steady hum of its generator lulled us to sleep.

It was with us until April when a large RAF lorry bore it away. The crew came to say goodbye and Vince returned to see us once or twice during the early summer, until he was posted abroad.

Every three weeks I took Brownie to the farrier on my way home from the round. Except for the pangs of hunger at having my dinner further delayed I enjoyed these visits to the forge. The farrier was a genial fellow. He talked about his work as he heated the iron in the glowing fire and hammered it into shape on the anvil. I watched as he trimmed Brownie's hooves and fitted the hot shoe while acrid yellow smoke rose to the rafters. While he hammered in the nails he asked me how I liked my job, the long hours and being out all weathers. I said it was worth it all for the freedom of the outdoor life. When he had finished I paid him three half-crowns for a full set of shoes.

Evenings were spent in front of the log fire, with Joy, the boss and his family recounting the events or discussing the problems of the farming day.

"Never," said the boss's wife, "does a farmer talk about anything else!" which was largely true, for farming is so much more than a job… it is a way of life.

One evening the boss asked me if I would like to come with him to the railway station where he had to deliver a churn of milk. We went out into the semi-darkness. Already the days were lengthening, giving a promise of light evenings to come.

"Like to drive?" asked the boss. "It's a pity not to keep in practice".

I took the wheel and had just got accustomed to the different gears and engine by the time we reached the road. We had not gone very far when, straight ahead, we saw a torch waving to and fro. As I pulled in and stopped the torch bearer came to the car window.

"There's a dead forest pony in the middle of the road", he warned us. As we were conveniently near the kennels, the boss fetched the huntsman and whipper-in and the men dragged the pony into one of the buildings.

"I'd better take over now," said the boss when he returned. He had just started the engine when there was a resounding crash. The car lurched forward and the ten gallon churn hurtled from the back seat onto my head. When I had stopped seeing stars and stripes and pink balloons I found that a woman in a large car had driven into the back of the boss's little Ford. Her vehicle escaped with a dented bumper, but his was too damaged to drive away. The boss sent me back to the farm to report what had happened while he telephoned from the kennels for a breakdown lorry.

Still reeling from the impact of the churn, I started back in the dark on the mile and a half walk. The car was a 'write-off'. It was my first experience of how dangerous ponies could be on the road at night.

Although February was almost at an end it continued to live up to its name of 'Fill Dyke'. Every morning I set off on the round in driving rain which continued sometimes into the afternoon when kale cutting became a soaking and miserable job.

My land army mac, always inadequate, was useless in this sort of weather. I sacrificed the last of my clothing coupons and bought a thick, double raincoat with a good wrap-over. This did keep me dry, although it got terribly wet doing it and in spite of hanging all night by the wash house fire it was still soggy in the morning.

"Aah", said Joe, when I complained about the continual downpour. "Yer wants t' do the round when 'tis snowing".

I didn't, especially.

"T' snow get in balls in t' pony's feet and 'er comes down. Then you 'as t' sit on 'er 'ead t' stop 'er gettin' up while you gets 'er out of the shafts".

I wondered how I was to get Brownie out of the shafts while sitting on her head.

"Of course ef you're on yer own, you'd 'ave t' set on 'er 'ead til help comes."

If such a catastrophe overtook me in the isolation of the Weirs, I envisaged myself sitting on Brownie's head in a snowstorm for some considerable time.

"Mind, she do tend t' go down on 'er knees anytime, 'specially downhill. Yer wants t' watch out fer thet".

Somehow conversations with Joe never inspired me with much confidence.

Potato harvesting.

CHAPTER 5

Percy & Joey

"Yer wants t'- wrap up". boomed Joe one morning, as I brought Brownie and float to the dairy door. "Wind's gone right round." It certainly whistled chillingly round the corner of the buildings, a foretaste of what it would be like across the Weirs.

"Tis a lazy wind" he continued, as we heaved up the big churn. "Don't go round ee, do go straight through!"

I thought as I set off on the round that one of those long awaited Land Army greatcoats would have come in handy. True as the old adage "When the days grow longer the cold grows a stronger" may be, once March and the lighter evenings arrive and the hazel catkins and celandines appear in the woods, the countryman or woman is warmed by the thoughts of Spring.

Now that the East winds had dried the fields work went ahead on preparing the land for spring sowing. The boss taught me to drive the older of the two Fordson tractors. The tuition, as with the pony driving, was merely a matter of showing me the basics. He rode with me for one turn of the field, having indicated the very simple working of the machine; a foot lever which was both brake and clutch, the throttle and gears. The exhaust belched out of a tall pipe at the side of the bonnet and blew into the driver's face if the wind was the wrong way; there were cleats on the iron wheels which gave extra grip on soft ground but a liver shaking ride over hard surfaces; the seat was of iron, without springs, but a folded sack slightly alleviated the discomfort. A beginner's greatest difficulty was selecting the gears without grinding, screaming protests from the box resounding across the fields.

After this brief introduction to the tractor I hitched on the disc harrows and pulled them up and down the field which had been ploughed after the kale. Bray, who had attached himself to me to an embarrassing degree and could barely be restrained from following me on the milk round, ran alongside hour after hour, often performing terrifying leaps across the drawbar between the tractor and the sharp blades of the discs. As the days lengthened we went on working after tea and when we had housed our tractors there was always the fascinating pastime of egg hunting. The hens, which had free range round the farmyard, seemed to vie with each other over the originality of their nesting sites, and collecting the eggs resembled a treasure hunt. One laid in the bonnet of an old car; another in the granary on top of a sack; we clambered over machinery in the cart shed to find one in a disused seed drill and climbed a ladder to one more, carefully laid on a folded tarpaulin in the straw barn. There was no end to their ingenuity or to our acrobatic feats performed in locating their nests.

We occasionally supplied eggs to a few special customers on the round. Fresh farm eggs to supplement the government ration were as precious as gold dust and carefully eeked out three at a time. One morning I took a long promised few for an Army major at the Balmer Lawn. I met him walking down the path from his office.

"Your eggs, Major," I exclaimed, holding them triumphantly aloft. The next moment they lay scrambled at his feet!

Now that the forest paths were no longer water logged I took a short cut home from the round along a woodland path called "the cover". Opposite the Balmer Lawn I left the road and drove across the green, through the enclosure gate into a belt of oaks that divided the farm fields. The path ran parallel with a wide stream crossed at one place by a rustic bridge. It was a place of enchantment where the ground blushed with pink wood anemones. Never, elsewhere, had I seen this delicate flower so abundant or so deep a colour. Primroses too, leaned over the banks and peered at their reflections in the clear stream.

Once in the cover I was happy to let Brownie amble, forgetting even the pangs of hunger in the charm of this tranquil spot. Now that spring in all its magic was here, every day on this forest farm brought a new delight. Only one thing was still needed to make it perfect. As yet I had not been able to get any riding. Then one day the boss told me that Jack, the huntsman, had a horse he would lend me. That evening I walked over to the kennels. I had met Jack briefly once before when he had been exercising the hounds in the wood. He was a small, wiry man, ruddy complexioned, the skin tight drawn over the prominent bones of his face. His deep blue eyes twinkled with humour. A man of rapid movement and dynamic energy, he was kind and generous but impatient of sloth or stupidity. He had a deep knowledge and understanding of horses and hounds and of the New Forest. Of the many memorable characters I met during my life on the land, Jack Slightam was perhaps the foremost. As I reached the stable yard he came from the flesh house, walking with his brisk, rapid stride and greeting me with a broad smile.

"Ah, you've come about the horse. Well, I've had this one in to put down, but I won't need him for a while and he's a decent sort – just suit you. You can keep him over at the farm and ride him when you like."

He led me to a small paddock where a bay gelding was grazing. He whickered and came over, a friendly horse with a large, kind eye. As I fondled him I had mixed feelings. Pleasant as it would be to have him to ride, I knew I would get very fond of him and all the while it would be on borrowed time. Jack intuitively divined my thoughts.

"Don't you worry about me taking him. I won't do that until I have to, not 'til we start hunting at the earliest. You take him m'dear, and enjoy your riding."

"What's his name?" I asked.

"We call him Percy," said Jack.

Percy was equipped with a bridle only. While I put it on him Jack bustled in the tack room looking out a suitable saddle and fitting it up with leathers and irons. Then I rode back to the farm. After that, I spent most of my leisure hours on Percy, getting to know him and the forest. He was a companionable, willing horse and a comfortable ride. He had an endearing habit, when I came off him (which I did quite frequently at first) of coming back for me, and if I was not already on my feet, gently nudging me with his nose. My falls were due chiefly to his one bad habit; shying violently and unpredictably.

My favourite ride lay through the yard gate, out of the New Park Enclosure and right handed along the enclosure fence. Having jumped a big fallen beech we followed the path by a winding stream to Queen's Bower. Here, where three streams meet, is a little bridge and on the other side the woods open out onto Black Knoll Heath. A canter along the pony tracks brought us to an open green near Brockenhurst Bridge and so home. Another route covered the rich beech woods of New Park Enclosure beyond which long marshy 'bottoms' run between the heaths and leading up from these, smooth green lightly wooded slopes 'the lawns'. Here we would pause while I enjoyed the view of heath and woodland.

Just before Easter, the pleasant even tenor of our days was disrupted by the arrival of two farm pupils. There had been several pupils on the farm in the past, all of whom seem to have been called 'Dick' and all of whom had left behind some possession to be collected at an indefinite future date. In the cupboard in my room was a 12 bore shotgun, a tweed jacket and a holdall – each belonging to one 'Dick' or another.

Alec was the first to arrive. He was no stranger to the family having spent all his vacations on the farm while at Reading University. He appeared to have a long-standing friendship with Joy. A big fellow with a fresh complexion and a mop of curling brown hair, he had an easy charm and a penchant for practical jokes which he carried off with an air of complete innocence. A few days later, at tea, we were joined by Richard, a tall, slim young man, the most notable feature of his lean, tanned face were the large penetrating dark eyes which regarded us girls with supercilious disdain. Because of a wonted silence, we decided that he was either shy or unsociable, but after a few days he became friendly with Alec, for both young men were waiting to join the RAF as trainee pilots. He continued to ignore us, however, except for frequent derogatory remarks about our capabilities and the presence of 'females about the place'. We worked hard and, we considered, efficiently and although we accepted Alec's light-hearted banter we could not tolerate Richard's persistent male chauvinism. In time he vented most of his hostility upon me. Having discovered my dislike of the farm cats he took a delight in shutting one or another of the unattractive bunch in my bedroom, so that each time I entered I would find Millie curled up on my pillow, or Mousie ensconced on the dressing table. Not that I disliked cats in general, but these were not only skinny and evil eyed, but extremely bad mannered, getting on the table at mealtimes and even jumping onto our laps and snatching food from our plates. One night I found a dead adder in my bed, and had little doubt as to how it got there. But petty annoyances were forgotten during working hours. The spring sowing was all important. In the afternoons, our rounds done, Joy and I joined Alec and Richard in the field. While I rode the seed drill behind Richard's tractor, Joy harrowed and rolled.

The days were fine and the nights clear. In brilliant moonlight we often worked far into the night. It was a different world; the silver lit field surrounded by shadowy woods; the dark shapes of the tractors; the occasional ghostly white shape of a barn owl drifting over the hedges. Each night grew chillier, or so it seemed to me on my high seat. Richard, glancing at me as we stopped to refill the drill, fetched a sack from his tractor. "Put this round your shoulders" he said brusquely, "and don't look so cold."

Surprised at this unusual solicitude I pinned the sack in place with my Land Army badge and appreciated the warmth. The simple hessian sack was often a source of comfort as an extra garment, to sit on, or to put over the back of a sick animal to keep it warm. Although they have several uses there is not much comfort to be had from today's blue plastic bag.

One night there was a white frost so severe that it nipped the buds of the oak trees and they remained bare all summer. But in spite of cold mornings, everywhere were the harbingers of spring. The house martins were building in the eaves above my bedroom window and when the young hatched I awoke to their chatter each morning. The windows consisted of a single pane which pushed out horizontally, forming a perfect target for the little white bottoms. Soon it was impossible to see through the glass but this was a small price to pay for the enchantment of seeing their tiny heads peering over the edge of the nest as the busy parents flew in and out.

Another spring job was the harrowing of the winter wheat. "It's odd," I remarked to the boss, "When you sow a lawn you keep off it carefully, but when a field of wheat is coming up you go over and over it with tractor and harrow and roller."

"That's right," he agreed. "But the more you go over wheat the better it likes it and pressing it down well keeps out the wire worm."

It was at 5 o'clock teatime that the farm work of the day was discussed: what had gone wrong with humorous or disastrous results, occasionally what had gone right; the tasks and prospects for the morrow, for this was the only meal at which we were all present. Breakfast, Richard and I had together before I left for my round and he to work on the arable, then the others came in one at a time from milking. At dinnertime Joy and I were always later than the others while bread and cheese supper was on the board for each to partake as they came in from overtime or leisure pastime.

But at tea-time we all collected round the big dining-room table. The boss sat a the head, breadboard, knife and a large wholemeal loaf beside him, cutting it as required and tossing inch thick slices across the table onto our plates as they became empty, and now and then, one in the direction of Bray who sat, ears pricked expectantly, tail gently sweeping the floor, at a discreet distance. With ravenous appetite the boys would each eat six to eight of these jumbo slices, us girls maybe four or five, spread with margarine and jam, sparingly because of rationing, and washed down with copious cups of tea. Sometimes there was home-made quince jam, with a tart taste and rough texture which I still remember.

I cannot think that these somewhat primitive habits would have suited the boss's wife and daughter. Maybe they had their private plate of thinly cut bread and butter.

In April the first issue of the Land Army's own magazine was published. Entitled *The Land Girl*, it appeared monthly, priced 3d, and soon reached a circulation of 21,000 copies. Over the years it provided an excellent record of all aspects of Land Army life. It began with an interesting editorial, then an article by an eminent personage such as the Minister of Agriculture in office at the time. There were letters, articles and poems by members, some lyrical, some hilarious. The hallmark of the Land Girl was her sense of humour, an essential characteristic. There was news of the WLA from all over Britain, from the Land Army in Scotland, in Northern Ireland and the Isle of Wight. There were excellent photographs of girls working at every sort of job on the land. There was the shepherdess; some girls took charge of a flock and spent long, cold winter nights in the lambing pens; surprisingly some showed great zeal for poisoning rats; others were employed in land reclamation, operating excavators with the big 'grab'; some formed threshing gangs; some took great pride in layering hedges and actually enjoyed wading knee deep in icy water clearing ditches; they thatched ricks. Ten thousand girls were engaged in horticulture. Girls were encouraged to take correspondence courses and take proficiency tests; they took part in ploughing matches and took care of prize stock and heavy horses. Photographs appeared of Her Majesty the Queen, Patron of the WLA, talking to girls at their work; at the Goldsmiths Hall in 1940 when Land Workers gathered from every county and four from the Scottish Land Army; and at Buckingham Palace where, on the fourth birthday of the WLA, Her Majesty entertained 300 representatives and members to tea.

A visit from Mrs Eleanor Roosevelt to a WLA Hostel in Warwickshire was followed by gifts from the USA, including one of £17,000 and ten wedding dresses – which delighted some Land Army brides. The money provided three Rest Break Houses and a new London Club. All this we learned from *The Land Girl* with news of Clubs run by WLA representatives, the YWCA or Young Farmers, which provided dances, concerts and lectures. Joy and I shared a copy. It gave us a whole new concept of the Land Army. It had the effect of making me feel very humble. In comparison with the feats of work I read about, my own contribution seemed very insignificant.

Soon it was May, that most lush month of all the year. Tall fronds of bracken reared their heads between the golden furze. There was a haze of bluebells in the cover beneath the beeches' pellucid green. The forest mares had dropped their foals and they ran on wobbly legs beside their dams.

Percy was looking handsome in his summer coat, the colour of a horse chestnut, and he was fit from regular exercise and good grazing.

"I like the look of your nag, Jo," said Richard one evening, when to my surprise he joined me as I walked home across the fields. It was the first conversational remark he had made to me and I responded by telling him about Percy. We chatted happily and easily then, about horses and his riding in Devon, where he had been a pupil for a year, until, in an unguarded moment I suggested that he must try Percy. He replied that he would like to very much. A few days later, when I went to fetch the horse for my usual Sunday afternoon ride, instead of coming to me as he usually did he was reluctant to be caught. Then I noticed the dried sweat on his withers and a saddle mark on his back.

I found Richard getting in the cows.

"I had your nag out this morning," he said casually.

"So I see, and you rode him jolly hard" I replied, "He's not fit for me to take out this afternoon."

"You see, I met these chaps going colt hunting and tagged along," he explained. "Percy's jolly good at it – he enjoyed it."

At certain times of the year the owners of ponies turned out on the forest round them up for branding or to get them in for breaking. Anyone with a horse can join in. It involves some hard riding over rough ground. In a few well chosen words I told him what I thought of someone who took my horse on an operation like colt hunting without permission and turned him out with the saddle mark on him. He grinned, unimpressed, and I thought that he would probably take Percy where and when he felt inclined.

"Oh, how I hate you!" I hissed, my fit of temper only serving to amuse him more. When I went upstairs to change out of my jodphurs I found the ugliest tom cat asleep in the middle of my bed. Venting my spleen on the unlucky feline, I seized it unceremoniously by the scruff of the neck and tossed it onto the landing, hoping as I did so that the RAF would need Richard soon. My wish was granted temporarily, for the next week he departed with other members of the Air Training Corps, to which he belonged, to spend a few days at a bomber command station.

Alec had returned to Reading some weeks before and the farm household returned to the peace we had known before the arrival of those two tiresome young men. Three days later, returning from my round I was surprised to see Richard sitting on the gate to the cover, elbows on knees, contentedly smoking the pipe which he usually sucked upside-down and empty, tobacco being scarce during the war. He got down and opened the gate for me to drive through. Not thinking that his presence there had anything to do with me, I thanked him and drove on, leaving him standing there. At his shout of indignation I pulled up.

"Damn it, Jo, I've been waiting half-an-hour to ride up with you!" he said, jumping into the float and taking the reins from me in his usual masterful fashion, while I sat down with some surprise on a bottle crate.

"How was Bomber Command?" I asked.

"It was great!" He proceeded to tell me enthusiastically all about the visit. "There was a jolly casual atmosphere though, not really what I'd expected."

"I suppose they have to relax in between."

"They're a grand lot of chaps. Gosh, Jo, I hope I get my wings!"

"I'm sure you will."

"I wish I was sure. It means a hell of a lot of swotting. Alec, lucky devil, has no problem. Passed his maths 98% or something like that."

I reflected that Richard, with his calm common sense, dedication and sometimes exasperating coolness could be better pilot material than Alec, who had the brains but a more mercurial temperament. Then I gave him the farm news. Mousey had a new litter of kittens; I was to have a new pony for the round and Brownie was to be retired; and the chief item, Sam, the cowman's son, had found a German flying helmet in the turnip field and there was a general alert for an enemy airman.

"I suppose everyone is on edge expecting him to pop up somewhere."

There was a certain apprehension on the farm while the enemy airman was at large. Joy and I went together to collect eggs in the dim light of the loft and my heart missed a beat when something moved at the back of the cart shed when I pulled out the milk float – but it was only cats jumping off a pile of sacks. I did not loiter in the short cut when I drove home from the round.

The owner of the helmet was the chief topic of conversation among my customers, especial concern being felt for the elderly living alone. There was relief all round when he was picked up almost a week later near Lymington.

We did not see much of Richard and Alec during the next few weeks. The boss had taken over an acreage of parkland on the other side of the village to plough up and sow with arable crops. Richard and Alec departed after breakfast on their bicycles, armed against starvation with huge packs of sandwiches, returning at dusk, dusty, tired but full of enthusiasm for their new work environment.

Joy and I were longing to see this beautiful park and what the boys were up to. Late one hot, Saturday afternoon the boss was going to check their progress and take them a billy can of tea and said we could come along. Fifteen minutes drive later we parked in a tree lined lane, passed through a long, white gate into typical English parkland; acres of soft green turf broken by single or groups of magnificent beech and oak trees. The plough had already carved out brown strips on its smooth surface and one area had been turned over and harrowed. It seemed a sacrilege to cut up this ancient sward and disturb the roots of trees that may have stood for centuries, but there was a war on and food must come first.

Alec greeted us with his usual cheerful grin but Richard was in a bad temper.

"It's been one hell of a day!" he burst out. "Sweltering hot! I've had the harrows tangled in tree roots twice, I've got a cracking headache and that blasted cuckoo hasn't stopped: 'Cuckoo, cuckcoo cuck-bloody-uckoo' all day! Thank heaven I've finished this bit!"

I giggled unsympathetically. "Have some tea."

"If you've finished you may as well knock off," the boss said. "You can start sowing on Monday if the weather holds."

Placated by the tea and a large hunk of cake, Richard covered over his tractor and picked up his haversack.

"We'll walk back by the river," he said to me. "We can come out in the same lane."

He carried the boss's 12 bore, and shot a rabbit as we crossed the park.

"Plenty of these beggars. They'll have to go or we won't get any crops. Arthur Witcher gets busy most days with his ferrets and nets."

He handed me the rabbit while he let go the second barrel at another and missed. Then he strode on while I followed, carrying the rabbit like a sportsman's attendant. It was an old buck and heavy.

The river was not much more than a wide stream but clear and rippling and full of life below and above the water; darting small fish, hovering dragonflies and countless small birds. The air was vibrant with their song. Alders and willows overhung the water, while bluebells crowded to the edge and on the far side kingcups glistened gold.

We strolled along the narrow, uneven path. I was still carrying the rabbit and my arm ached. Suddenly Richard turned. "Here, give me that. I'd clean forgotten you were still lugging it. Now watch carefully, this is where I saw a kingfisher yesterday."

Richard had recovered his health and temper, for who could be out-of-sorts in such an enchanted place. We waited silently for a few minutes, to be rewarded by a flash of vivid blue.

"There you are! I wanted to bring you here Jo, I knew you'd love it. Come and see these sticklebacks…"

I smiled at his boyish enthusiasm and thought what a nice person he really was.

My new pony arrived. He was called Jerry, but Richard said this was unpatriotic, so we renamed him Joey. A smart little flea-bitten grey with pretty head and trim legs, he had been a childrens' hunter and had pulled a governess cart. A milk round must have been a social comedown and a lot harder work, so that I sympathised with his objections to being backed into the float even though he showed his ill temper by nipping my arm. Nor would he stand while I slid the shafts into the loops. Repeatedly backing him and lifting the shafts was consuming of time and patience and by the end of the week I had an array of assorted bruises from his strong teeth. I tried to enlist Joe's help but all he said was, "Aah, they all 'as their funny liddle ways. You'll get used to un." Which was all very well, I thought, when it was not his arm Joey was biting.

Once on the road Joey trotted on at a cracking pace and I got back from the round 45 minutes earlier. It was almost worth the morning tussle for the exhilaration of driving a fast pony and watching his flowing mane and tail, his small black velvety ears twitching to and fro, while the float sailed along like Boadicea's chariot. Then one day when I came out of a house there was no sign of Joey or the float. I followed a cloud of dust and a trail of broken bottles to the end of the road. Round the corner came a workman leading my errant pony.

"Just managed to stop 'im, Miss," he said, "'e weren't 'arf going!"

I thanked him and he helped me pick up the broken glass.

In the course of the next week several people, including a fellow roundsman and the village policeman, returned my pony to me. Then the boss had an idea. The next day I carried a 28lb weight in the float. This was attached to a line which passed through the rings of the harness to Joey's bit. I put down the weight at every stop. My customers were fascinated with the contrivance which they called my "anchor". For a while all was well on the round.

On the farm it was hoeing time again. My year had come full circle. Most of the hoeing was done by the Witcher family but I did not escape the field weeding.

Now you would not think that the most stupid female to put a leg into Land Army dungarees could go wrong with pulling docks out of a pasture. After the boss left me with this instruction I looked at the field in dismay. There were endless docks, especially small ones, but I set about painstakingly removing them all. I had cleared three parts of the ground of every trace of the spiked red flowers when the boss walked over to see how I was getting on. When he looked at my work his face showed none of the satisfaction I had expected.

"Good God, girl, you've pulled all the sorrel as well!" he exclaimed. How could I not have known the difference between docks and sorrel, which the boss went on to explain was of value as cattle feed. I had not only wasted time and effort, but robbed the cows of nutriment as well.

"Just what you would expect of a female!" scoffed Richard when the story of my mistake had been well circulated.

Meanwhile Joey continued to demonstrate his complete unsuitability as a milk pony, showing a tendency to bolt or shy at the least provocation. One of the last calls on my round was to the side door of a shop in the High Street, where I drove into a small yard. Owing to Joey's extreme unpredictability I always led him out into the traffic.

At the end of a long, hot morning in June when I was looking forward to my short lunch break and a cool drink, something spooked him in the yard and he charged at the gateway. The offside shaft hit the post and he reared straight up, coming down heavily on my right foot.

The urgent need to calm him probably lessened the first impact of intense pain, but on the way back to the Balmer Lawn pain took over and I drove in a daze. Luckily we did not meet an army lorry which Joey so much disliked and we arrived quietly and safely at the back of the building. As I limped tearfully to the kitchen to collect the empty churn I received some concerned attention from two young subalterns who were leaning out of an upstairs window and more sympathy from the ATS cooks. But it was their officer who took command.

"The foot must be X-rayed," she said. Quickly and authoritatively she telephoned the farm for someone to collect the milk float, then organized a car to take me to Lymington hospital where I spent an hour in casualty.

There was no fracture; even so, by the evening my foot was as swollen as a melon and the boss lent me an old carpet slipper, slit down the side.

Joe had not been pleased at having to fetch the float from the Balmer Lawn and was even less so about doing my round the next morning. But if I had envisaged a restful day on the sofa with my foot on a cushion it was swiftly dispelled.

"As you cannot do the round" said the boss, "you had better give the Whitchers a hand with the hoeing."

So after breakfast, still wearing the boss's slipper and using my hoe as a crutch, I hobbled out to the swede field, where Mrs Whitcher was all motherly concern.

"Now you sit down, dearie, and rest that pore foot," she said when I had done a turn of the field. "Me and 'enry will do a bit hextry and Connie will get some comfrey leaves to take out the swelling."

With frequent rests, I got through the day. After a night's rest and a poultice of Connie's comfrey leaves I was able to get my shoe on the next morning and do my round.

In mid-June, Joy and I joined a WLA outing – organised by Mrs Brown and another area representative – to The Vyne, near Basingstoke, then the family seat of the Chute family.

The coach, already filled with Land Girls, picked us up near the lodge gates at 1.30pm. Until I had met Joy, a few months before, I had not seen another Land Girl and it was quite an experience to find a whole coach load *en masse*. As we were 'out' and in uniform we all wore our hats and I was fascinated by what could be done with a plain, round brimmed, regulation hat. Some were porkpie style, some Anzac, up at the front, the back, and even one Annie Oakley, on the back of the head and tied with a bootlace under the chin! It was a long ride, almost across the county, but the afternoon was perfect, sunlight enhancing the lush green of tree foliage, grass and young corn; hedgerows decked with wild roses and honeysuckle, and fringed with cow parsley. We sat back and enjoyed this restful break from our usual routine.

My memories of The Vyne are of a long, two storey house with projecting wings, in beautiful rose red brick glowing in the sun; surrounded by spacious green lawns, on one side sloping down to a picturesque lake. We spent the afternoon walking round the grounds, conservatories and hothouses, had tea on the terrace and exchanged notes with other girls on our varied farm work. On the way home we passed a field cut for hay.

"We'll be haymaking next week," said Joy. And we were.

The weather remained fine for the whole of the hay harvest, three weeks of hot, cloudless days when the sweet scent of mown hay almost obliterated the smell of tractor fumes. The hay made quickly. Sam was out with the swath turner and Joy and I turned some with pitch forks. When it was ready to be carried we were in the field from the time we hurriedly ate our lunch until the dew fell, sometimes about nine o'clock, loading the carts and wagons. Two were pulled by the tractor and a third by the mare in the charge of Arthur. The rest of the Witcher family assisted in the loading or worked with the boss on the rick. A little excitement was provided by having both sides of the family in the same field. It arose when Arthur shouted at "lil' 'enry" probably in response to some cheek from the youngster. Mrs Witcher flew at him like a vixen defending her young. Henry senior joined in and soon pitch forks as well as voices were raised. "lil' 'enry" got in a sly kick to Arthur's shin but the timid Johnnie made no move to defend his father. Richard and Sam at last broke up the scuffle, which subsided into scowls and dark mutterings.

The heatwave continued. Day after day the sun shone and the temperature rose. It was still hot even when we had finished work for the day.

"Let's go for a swim before supper" Richard suggested one evening as we walked back to the house over the cleared field.

"Where?" I asked, thinking that the sea was a bit too far away for a pre-supper dip.

"In the stream, of course!"

Almost opposite the enclosure gate, the stream, by the banks of which I so often rode, widened and deepened into a pool. In the centre it was deep enough for diving from a jutting log. We dived and floated and swam lazily to and fro while the cold water eased our aching muscles. Then we sat on the log with our feet in the water and talked until the gnats discovered us and we beat a rapid retreat.

The hot dry weather that was so good for the hay adversely affected the milk yield and every day I had to finish the round in the afternoon. Being put into harness for a second time in the day put Joey thoroughly out of temper and one morning he decided to show me what he could really do in the way of bolting. It was on the way home, on Brockenhurst Bridge, that we met the first of a convoy of army lorries. Joey threw up his head and quickened his trot but I managed to keep him in hand. Then came the little trucks with their flapping canvas roofs. I felt his hindquarters tuck under him as he leapt into a gallop. With his head held straight up until he appeared to be looking at the sky rather than at the road ahead, he careered past the turning to the cover and continued up the main road at an alarming pace while lorries and trucks flicked by. He had the bit firmly between his teeth and there was no stopping him. He took the turning into the farm drive without slackening speed, the float on one wheel. We missed the gate post by the lodge by inches and scraped the corner of the granary building. Then at the dairy door he stopped dead and stood as quietly as a cab horse as if nothing had occurred. Having once got away with me Joey's bolting became a regular habit. The strain proved too much for the well worn harness. One day a trace broke; a few days later a rein, luckily the right one, and I pulled him over to the left into a wood where he stopped amid the trees.

"What he needs is a driving martingale," said Jack. "Stop him getting his head up."

I mentioned it to the boss. "We'll see about it" he replied but there the matter ended. He probably thought, like Joe, that there was nothing wrong with the pony. It was just that "Gals never could 'andle 'orses". After a while I came to regard the mad dashes up the main road, the hair raising turns into the drive and the near misses of gate posts and walls as just part of my daily routine.

As his bolting only occurred on the way home I thought they might be more from mischief than fright and his next trick convinced me. At the end of the cover I had to get down to open the field gate. Joey did not wait for me to get up again. He was through in a flash, cantering across the field, churns, crates and bottles jangling, while I was left to trudge behind picking up the bottles that had bounced out of the crates.

"I wish you didn't have to drive the damn pony. You'll get hurt," said Richard with genuine concern. I thought how much he had changed. We had lengthening periods of truce and an increasing enjoyment in each other's company.

The good weather broke at the end of the only heatwave in what turned out to be the wettest summer of the war. The morning after the last of the hay was carried we awoke to the sound of teeming rain which continued all day.

"You youngsters may as well have the afternoon off," said the boss, looking out at the downpour. "You all deserve a break".

I wondered how to spend a free wet afternoon. I could cycle home but it was a daunting thought; Percy would be too wet to put a saddle on, so I could not ride. In the end I decided to catch up with some letters and some sock mending. In a weak moment I had volunteered to mend Richard's socks as well and he kept me well supplied. There was a pile awaiting my attention. On my way upstairs to fetch them I met Richard.

"Come to the pictures, Jo?" he asked, "There's a film in Southampton about Bomber Command that I want to see." It was a more attractive proposition than sock mending.

"I'd like to," I said.

"I'm afraid we'll have to hitch hike," he told me, when, having fetched a mac and headscarf, I joined him in the yard.

"I haven't had my pocket money from home this month and I've only enough cash for the tickets."

"I've only got 1/6d." I said, "But the boss owes me some money."

My wages were one of the little things the boss was absent minded about, but as he did not deduct my board and lodging and remembered to pay me eventually, I seldom reminded him. I had little need of money in my present mode of life.

"I shouldn't worry, as long as you don't mind a bit of walking in the rain."

"I'm used to rain," I said.

Once on the road, our hopes of a lift seemed optimistic. There was very little about except for the army trucks and lorries. We walked about a mile on the verge under weeping skies and dripping trees. Then a little grey car pulled up and two grey heads appeared at the windows.

"Like a lift?" cried the two elderly occupants. Gratefully we climbed in.

Our driver and companion chatted gaily to us. Finding that they had some petrol left they had decided to go for a drive before getting the next month's ration. They took us to within a mile of Southampton, where we thanked them and left them, not a little amused at these two sweet old ladies driving around the countryside in the rain to use up their petrol ration.

The film was a good one about the flying operations of the crew of a Wellington bomber. When we came out it was still raining. Turning up our collars we started walking, discussing the film and not too disheartened by the number of cars that passed us by. Two miles further on a lorry stopped. I climbed into the high cab between Richard and the burly driver, smiling a little at the contrast from our first lift. It took us as far as Lyndhurst. The Brockenhurst road was now deserted and we settled down to the last wet miles home, sometimes talking, sometimes in companionable silence. After one of these Richard suddenly said; "I wish we had another horse, Jo, so that we could ride together. I suppose the boss wouldn't let you ride Joey?"

"It doesn't seem fair to ride a hard working pony on his time off," I replied doubtfully.

"Maybe he wouldn't have the spare energy to bolt so much if you did," Richard suggested.

That, I thought, was a good point. I would ask the boss.

Stooking corn.

CHAPTER 6

Riding & Falling

I did not turn Joey out after the Sunday morning round but fed him and left him in the stable as the boss had given me permission to ride him that afternoon.

"But only this once, mind," he said. "It's not to become a habit."

Richard got Percy in so that we could saddle up straight away after lunch. 'Saddle up' only applied to Percy, for there was no tackle to fit Joey, so I rode him bareback with a halter.

We went our favourite way, out of the enclosure gate by the fallen beech. Joey went flying over it after Percy, and I was surprised to find myself still with him on the other side. Through the trees we glimpsed the encampment of the Witcher family; a group of tents through a haze of wood-smoke; tethered ponies and sleeping dogs. Further on we met Mrs Witcher and Connie gathering firewood. Mrs Witcher was a wizened little woman clad in a long black dress with a black hat pulled down over her grey hair. She was usually quiet and rather timid, keeping close to her spouse, except on Saturday nights when she drove home from the local inn standing up in the trap urging on the pony to a spanking trot, a veritable Boadicea with her two daughters behind her.

I was on excellent terms with the gypsies, especially with Connie who, on my days off, would come early to the back door with a bunch of woodland flowers picked with the dew on them, for me to take home to my mother: bluebells with wood spurge, then honeysuckle with red campion, cow-parsley and dog roses. They filled the saddlebag of my bicycle.

Arthur was abroad too, that afternoon, rabbiting. He stopped to show us his ferret, delving to the bottom of a deep sack and producing the soft cream-coloured animal.

"Nice ferret that, Miss. Lucy, I calls 'er. Only six weeks old. Quiet as a kitten she is." He let the ferret crawl round his neck and shoulders to demonstrate her docility. Joey eyed her with apprehension.

"There, Miss, quiet as a kitten. Good worker too, and only six weeks old."

"Jolly nice, Arthur," said Richard, moving on. "Hope you get plenty of rabbits."

"Aah yes, she's a good little ferret…" Arthur went on, extolling Lucy's merits until we were out of earshot.

We rode on toward Queen's Bower. Joey was keen but manageable. For over an hour we walked and trotted under the trees, or cantered across the heath and along soft turf rides between the bracken. It was on the way home that I got the sensation of numbness in my legs. I had only ridden bareback for very short distances until now, and it was getting increasingly difficult to hang on. Richard on Percy was still cantering ahead and my shouts for him to stop fell on deaf ears. At last I chose a comfortable looking piece of turf and rolled off, but because of the speed that Joey was travelling I did not land quite where I intended and hit my head on a tree stump. When I got up two rather blurred ponies were careering through a great many trees after a couple of Richards on two Percys. Richard stopped at last, caught Joey and brought him back to me. "What made you fall off?" he asked in surprise.

"It was deliberate," I replied. "My legs couldn't take any more."

"You should have called out. I'd have pulled up."

"I did," I said.

"You'd better take Percy. I'll ride Joey home and we'll take it gently."

It was a relief to be in a saddle again. Richard riding Joey looked slightly comical with his long legs almost to the ground.

"Are you all right?" he asked as an afterthought.

"Umm, except that every time I look at you you're twins."

I was still seeing double and feeling distinctly queasy when we reached the farm. Leaving Richard to turn out the horses I went to bed.

In spite of its ending it had been a wonderful afternoon and I was sorry that I would not be allowed to ride Joey again. Oddly enough it was through the pony that I found a horse for Richard.

One of the far flung outposts of my milk round was a large house on the further side of the Weirs, the home of a retired Colonel who must once have kept several horses, for there was a block of stables behind a big paddock. In addition to dropping my 'anchor', I always tied Joey onto the fence here, for had he decided to bolt he could have gone for miles across the forest. The morning after the ride I came out of the gate to find that something had indeed spooked him. He had pulled back suddenly from the fence and his snaffle bit had broken through at the link and was hanging from his mouth in two pieces. I looked at it in dismay. We were still six miles from home and the thought of leading him that distance was daunting. I had not met the Colonel, but now I saw him pottering in his garden. He looked a little incredulous at my story of the broken bit but quickly led the way to his tack room, and after a short search found a bar snaffle that would fit Joey's bridle. In a few moments I was ready to drive. After I had thanked him I admired a handsome grey cob grazing in the paddock.

"Old Sultan? Oh, he does nothing. Just eating his head off. I wish I could find someone to exercise him."

I hesitated only a moment, then told him about Richard: "...and we'd very much like to borrow a horse so that we can ride together," I concluded. "All right, splendid! Send him along to see me and we'll see what we can arrange."

The result was that the following Sunday afternoon Richard set off from the farm on his bicycle for the Weirs and Sultan while I saddled Percy and rode across Black Knoll Heath to meet him. We rode back over the brilliance of heather and gorse and white pony tracks into the tenebrous shade of the enclosure and out again onto expanses of bracken now tall as our horses' withers, where the fallow does hide young new born kids in its shelter. Small details added to the charm of the summer afternoon: the sudden flash of a rabbit's white scut against a patch of crimson ling; a comma butterfly feeding on the blackberry blossom. Richard seemed very pleased with his mount and this was the first of several pleasant rides together, but soon riding was superseded by a fresh interest.

"Care to come and look at some sheep, Jo?" asked Richard one teatime.

As Percy had cast a shoe, leaving me with nothing better to do, I agreed.

"Where *are* these sheep?" I enquired as we got out our bicycles.

"On the golf course."

Brockenhurst Golf Course was a mile or more the other side of the village. As we cycled along Richard told me that the flock of three hundred sheep belonged to the local butcher. They were being looked after by a friend of the boss, Bob McGee, and his wife Diana.

"Bob is a sick man but the doctors thought the life would be good for him. He can't do much work, obviously. His wife helps, but all the foot rot and maggots since the rain is too much for them to cope with. The boss suggested that I could give them a hand."

"Do you know much about sheep?"

"Used to work with the flock in Devon. I thought you would like to come along for company."

This, I discovered, was his euphemistic way of involving me in an evening of hard work.

First we met Bob, an elderly grey haired Scot and his tall, attractive wife who was many years younger than he. Leaving our bikes by the caravan we walked with them to look for the sheep which, with the usual perversity of that animal, were at the far end of the golf course.

Now sheep will follow the shepherd they know, and his dog will round up the stragglers, but we were complete strangers to this flock and we had no dog. That is where I came in. It turned out I had a whole new potential as a sheepdog. Even so, it took some time to get the three hundred head into pens that had been put up by the railway fence that formed one boundary of the course. Then there were the inevitable few that turned-tail by the hurdles and bolted in the direction they had come. Finally, with Diana's help, we got them all in to the last recalcitrants, having carefully counted them and all made a different number. We decided to take Bob's count as it was the one we wanted.

"How can you count them when they are tumbling through in woolly bundles of three and four at a time?" I asked.

"Och, it's parfectly simple," laughed Bob. "Ye count their legs and divide by four!"

There were, in fact, three hundred and a half sheep, for one ewe had given birth to a late lamb in the lorry and miraculously it survived, if somewhat grubby, to be tenderly cared for by Diana, who named it Lottie. She made a pen for it and its dam and the little ewe lamb became a pet.

We stood looking at the rest of the flock.

"There are several lame ones," Richard observed, "and some fly backs. Let's get to work!"

We picked out the lame sheep and drove them through to a second pen.

"Now, to throw a sheep on its back," Richard instructed me, "you grasp its back and front leg on the side nearest you and pull it over…"

This sounded simple enough, but at my first try something went wrong and it was not the sheep that landed on its back.

"Good show chaps!" applauded Richard. "Try again."

This time I got it right, then leant on the poor beast to keep it still while Richard cut away the rotten hoof and brushed on Stockholm Tar from the tin I held. I was not very heavy and sheep are very strong. A brief, unguarded moment on my part and a sudden heave on hers and sheep, myself, the pot of tar and brush parted in divers directions.

Today, the shepherd uses not a knife and tar on rotting feet but an efficient pair of clippers and an aerosol, antiseptic spray. He catches the sheep's leg in his crook and seemingly with a mere flick of the wrist has it sitting comfortably between his legs where he carries out its pedicure unaided. But this was 1941 and we were enthusiastic amateurs.

We worked through the evening, the hours marked by the passage of a little engine which chugged busily along the line with a volume of smoke and an air of importance inapposite to its load of two coaches. When the train had passed three times and the sun had set we had only the few sore backs to attend to. The flies lay their eggs under the sheep's wool and the maggots, when they hatch, eat into its flesh leaving it red and raw. We washed these places with diluted Jeyes Fluid and daubed them with Stockholm tar. As dusk fell we turned out the flock and tired, dirty and reeking of Jeyes and tar, walked back to the caravan.

"Come on in," cried Diana, who had preceded us. "Come and have a wash and some supper."

We accepted gratefully.

"Look, I've just picked these on one of the greens." She showed us a small basketful of mushrooms. "I'm going to fry them with some bacon."

"We shouldn't eat your bacon ration," I said.

Diana grimaced and put some rashers in the pan. Soon the delicious aroma of bacon and mushrooms heightened our appetite.

As we ate them with thick slices of fried bread and drank coffee, Bob and Diana talked of the sheep and farming, of horses and the riding establishment they had kept in Devon. Bob, whose long illness had not quenched his droll Scottish humour and the vivacious Diana kept up a lively flow of stories and anecdotes about the rural scene. Outside the caravan darkness and stillness fell except for the calling of owls and distant bleating of the sheep.

It was the first of many such evenings. The damp humid weather bred foot rot and maggots and there was work for us at least twice a week. Maggots, which were often to be found round the tail area where the wool was soiled, were not so easy to detect as the sore backs, so we examined each one as they passed through the hurdles, separating those afflicted. Then we cut away the wool round the affected place and poured on Jeyes Fluid. I took a sadistic delight in watching the squirming dying maggots pour out of the flesh as the Jeyes got to them.

"Nature must have been in a foul mood when she made parasites," I said. "They're disgusting!"

As each sheep got up and shook itself, relieved of its tormentors, I felt that we had done a good job.

Lottie was growing well and running free now with her dam. Lottie gambolling round the ewe, pirouetting off an ant hill, or just putting her head round the caravan door was a frequent source of amusement. We worked with the sheep until it was too dark to see, then sat over supper with the McGees, each night a little longer, often not returning to the farm until everyone had gone to bed. As we gently opened the back door, Bray, who knew our footsteps, gave us a silent greeting and we stealthily climbed the stairs, hoping not to wake the boss who would then warn us at breakfast about burning the candle at both ends.

But those were the days of youth and endless vitality. Late nights and early mornings bothered us not at all. Richard frequently burned the midnight oil swotting for his Air Force examinations. When farm work was at its peak he joined the Home Guard and somehow fitted in those duties as well.

At the end of July when Alec arrived for the long summer vacation, Mrs Gough told me that she could not cope with looking after five young people and I must find a billet elsewhere.

I was dismayed at having to leave the farmhouse and shocked when I found that no other billet was available. The local Land Army representative combed the village without success.

"Unless the Witcher family have a spare tent, "I said to Richard, "I shall have to get another job."

"I don't want you to go, Jo, I shall miss you."

I would miss him too – more than I cared to admit – the others, too, and the Slightams, and not least of all, Percy.

"It's a shame you're going," said Alec, adding his commiseration, "now that we've got to know you. You've changed. You used to be so sedate when you first came."

"Sedate!" I echoed.

"You were, you know. But you're quite different now."

I hoped I was not too different, that with my new found exuberant spirits I had not become over abandoned, like a calf turned out to grass. My appearance had changed, too. Almost a stone heavier, strong and permanently tanned, I now looked a veritable daughter of the soil. The last few months had undoubtedly had the greatest influence on me, physically and emotionally, than any other time in my young life. Now it was coming to an end.

"There is one more place you could try," the boss suggested. "That's the kennel cottage. I don't hold out much hope, but you could ask."

Mrs Slightam said she was sorry, she did have a spare room, but it would be occupied by her nephew Jim when he came to whip in at the start of the hunting season. So that was that.

I was turning Percy out after riding him a few evenings later, feeling miserable that there would be few more rides, when Mrs Slightam's young son Johnnie came across the field.

"Mother would like to see you" he said.

Mrs Slightam met me at the cottage gate.

"Jack and I have talked about you staying here," she told me. "We have decided to do up the bothy for Jim. You can have his room if you still want to come."

If I still wanted to come! In my delight I could have hugged her.

CHAPTER 7

Summer & Romance

I moved to my new billet at the kennel cottage at the weekend. Immediately beneath my bedroom window was a green paddock, to the side of which lay the wide gravel drive which rounded the corner of the kennel buildings to the stables, yard and fleshhouse. Beyond lay the farm fields and the cover; to the right, trees hid the farmhouse and buildings from view but revealed a big, red brick house. Here lived one old lady, Miss Matthews, whom no-one ever saw and whom Joy and I regarded as a sort of latter-day Miss Haversham.

I brought Percy with me from the farm to graze in the paddock and every night for the first week Bray slipped away from the farmhouse and slept on the porch under my window, in spite of all my efforts to send him home. That first night and for many nights at the kennels I was awakened by the baying of hounds.

"Ah, that's hound music!" laughed Jack when I mentioned it. "The sweetest music in the world. You'll get used to it." But if the music turned to snarling or fighting among the pack, Jack would lean out of his bedroom window and shout once, and there would be instant silence.

When I came down in the morning Dot Slightham was cooking an appetising breakfast over a primus stove. As days passed I found that beneath the rather dour manner of this Dorset woman, was a kind and generous nature, a rich fund of wisdom and a keen sense of fun. I became very fond of her and she remained my good friend long after my Land Army days were over.

During the long light evenings I became integrated into the activities of the kennels, and I learned a lot.

"I'll teach you the proper way to groom a horse, my lady," said Jack one day, 'my lady' being his favourite mode of address to anything female, be it human, equine or canine, or occasionally bovine.

I watched him working briskly on a big bay gelding using a hard circular movement of the dandy brush, hissing loudly all the while between his teeth without pausing for breath.

"You hiss to keep the dust out of your mouth," he explained.

"But how do you breathe in when you're hissing out all the time?" I asked.

"Practice." he grinned. "Now you try…"

I took the brush and applied it, I thought, with the same firm circular movement, but Jack laughed.

"Don't tickle – brush!" he said, "and don't forget to hiss."

I watched him prepare the cut meat which was cooked in a huge copper, and mixed with barley meal, and the oat cakes that were fed dry. I saw him skim the cold fat off the cooked meat and put it into great barrels which went away for the manufacture of soap. I watched him working with the carcasses in the flesh house.

"Meat is getting short," he said. "We've had the otter hounds here for two weeks and don't they eat!"

I cast a wary eye upon Percy in the paddock.

"Don't you worry. I shan't take him!" Jack promised.

Then two pony road casualties and a dead heifer and calf relieved the situation. "Too much now all together" said Jack, "Just when Jim's away and I've no help with the skinning."

"Let me help," I offered. "You could teach me."

"All right my lady, I'll teach you!"

I started on the calf. It was much the same principal as skinning a rabbit, which I had done. Cutting up the belly and the inside of the legs, and pulling the skin toward myself while running the skinning knife between the skin and the flesh, being careful not to nick the hide.

When I went on to the pony Jack laughed at the expression of distaste on my face.

"I was afraid you wouldn't care for the stench!" he said. "I've just realised that you're not smoking. It helps."

"I've never smoked," I replied, "but if you puff hard at that pipe and blow the cloud this way I'll be all right."

"Perhaps you could give me a hand," said Mrs Slightam a few evenings later. "I'm going to train oil the hounds. Twice a year we rub them over with train oil and paraffin," she explained "It improves their coats and gets rid of any parasites."

Never happier than when handling animals, I was enjoying the task when I noticed Dot eyeing me strangely as I rubbed down one gaunt looking dog with a scarred face.

"I was interested to see what would happen there," she said when I had finished. "Old Rasper has never let anyone but Jack handle him before."

"Now you tell me!" I exclaimed.

"Oh, he wouldn't have bitten you – not without warning." She was right, I thought, not to warn me. Had she done so I would have been apprehensive and Rasper, sensing it, might not have been so amenable.

Involved in these new activities two weeks passed without seeing Richard. This was partly due to one of the past pupils called Dick spending a few days at the farm. I wondered if he had come to collect his gun or jacket, or holdall from the bedroom cupboard. He and Richard spent a lot of time together. Then one morning as I was loading up the float, Richard came from the cow pens. He stopped by the dairy door.

"Jo, I never see you these days!" he complained, setting down the pails of milk.

"I wanted to see you," I replied. "Mrs Slightam asked me if you would like to come to supper one night."

"Good show. When?"

"What about tomorrow if you've no ATC. About seven-thirty?"

"Fine. See you then," he said, pouring the milk into the cooler as I took out the last crate.

By 7.30 the next evening Mrs Slightam had prepared a supper of tinned pilchards, salad and bread and butter and opened a precious tin of fruit. We waited a little while but there was no sign of Richard. Half an hour went by and still he did not appear. It was impossible, I thought, that he could have forgotten anything to do with food.

"Look Jose," said Mrs Slightam at last, "Jack and I are going out. So if you don't mind we'll have ours. You can wait for Richard if you like."

They had just gone when Richard arrived, breathless and apologetic.

"A ruddy load of fertilizer arrived," he exploded, "just as I was coming out and not a darn soul about the place!"

"So you had to help unload it yourself."

"And I had to change my clothes twice!"

I commiserated on his bad luck, reflecting how often this sort of thing happened. A farmer or resident employee only had to be dressed and in the car ready to go to some social function for a cow to calve or something to occur which needed his immediate attention.

"We shan't have many more free evenings" Richard told me as we sat down. "The boss starts cutting the oats tomorrow. We shall be harvesting every night".

"I suppose it is about time," I replied, for the corn had been slow to ripen. The weather, when not actually wet, had been cool and sunless and although it was nearly August, very little corn had been cut.

When I drove off on the round next morning, the boss was getting out the binder. It seemed to me a curious thing about the British farmer that however long he had been waiting to start a job, he did not get out his machine and service it until the day he wanted to use it. On this occasion the binder needed only a morning spent on preparing it for use and when I came back from the round I heard the rumbling of its canvas with the drone of the tractor and the "clack-clack" as the sheaves were ejected. But before many rounds of the field had been completed down came the rain and did not clear before mid-morning the next day.

"You'd better go and stand up those sheaves that were cut yesterday," the boss told Joy and me. Somehow I had missed this job the previous year and Joy had to show me how to stand the sheaves in a row of four pairs, heads together, butts sufficiently far apart to balance and give a passage of air in between. Names for this operation varied according to the area: it was known as 'heiling' in the north, 'stooking' in Sussex and in Hampshire it was 'shocking'. Joy and I, handling the tall oat sheaves sodden from the night's rain, certainly got 'shockingly' wet. It was when shocking, too, that our fingers found all the thistles that had not been hoed out earlier in the year.

By tea time the standing corn had dried sufficiently for cutting to be resumed and the next morning it was still going well. Then at 2 o'clock as we all made ready to go out into the field again, came the deluge. We stood in the cart shed watching the growing puddles in the yard.

"I 'low we'll be harvestin' til Christmas," said Joe "ef et do go on like this!"

It did go on like that. Every day it dried enough for Richard and Alec to start cutting, only to be stopped again by rain that arrived with disconcerting punctuality in the early afternoon. The boss's mood was as gloomy as the weather and was reflected in the spirits of his employees.

It was while we were shocking the always wet sheaves that Mrs Witcher confided to me that she was 'expectin', "An' me past fifty!" she said proudly. Thinking of her age and her still older spouse and the dingy, overcrowded camp, I wondered if her news was a matter for congratulation, but she and Henry both seemed so delighted with their achievement that I had to offer mine.

"When is it to be?" I asked.

"I'm just six months gone," she told me, although under the voluminous black skirt there was as yet only a slight thickening of her skinny figure.

"Will you go into hospital to have the baby?"

"Lor no!" she exclaimed in horror, "Not one of them places. My cousin'll come over to look after me. She delivered the others."

I envisaged the baby being born in a smoke-filled tent in November and suppressed a shudder.

When the evenings were dry, but earlier rain had stopped corn carting, Richard and I still worked with the sheep. Alec and Joy, who spent their free evenings at the cinema in Lymington or the local hop, failed to understand our enthusiasm for this hobby.

"You can't really enjoy sitting on a sheep's back hacking away at foot rot!" they declared. But we had been very happy in our self-appointed task, although now there was an overtone of sadness. Bob was in hospital. We now knew that he had lung cancer and that he was dying. Diana stayed on at the caravan and did what she could with the sheep now joined by her nine-year-old daughter, also Diana, who was on holiday from boarding school. A delightful fawn eyed, honey-blonde child, she was nicknamed 'Dee-Two'.

Sometimes I went alone and tried to get the sheep in before Richard joined me after ATC, but there was little time then to work before dusk.

Having once been made welcome at the kennel cottage Richard often found his way there around supper time. This meal varied considerably, according to how the rations could be stretched and sometimes it was just bread and cheese and cocoa. These occasions were helped out by my agricultural ration of eight ounces of cheese. Richard and Alec complained bitterly that Joy and I, mere females, were allowed all this cheese, while they, who did all the heavy work (an assertion we disputed) but were not paid employees with an agricultural insurance stamp, were entitled to only a paltry two ounces each. Whatever the supper fare at the kennel cottage, the happy atmosphere and lively conversation never flagged. After I had cleared the table and Dot had lit the oil lamp, Jack would pull at his pipe and regale us with stories of the Forest and hounds and horses from his rich fund of experience. Incidents, some exciting, some amusing, a few catastrophic, were recounted. There was the time when a stag took to water and swam out to the middle of a large pond. Jack and Jim found an old boat moored in the bushes and rowed out to drive the stag ashore, only to be told by an old woodman who was waiting when they pulled in the boat, that it had not been untied for forty years!

There was the accident when the master broke his neck but recovered and Jack, himself suffered a broken leg when a rider slammed the gate on it at Hinchlea Lodge.

"Didn't feel a thing," he said, "until I came to dismount and saw it hanging loose in my boot."

He told us of the Boxing Day point-to-point race that was held every year before the war, from Telegraph Post to Picket Post. It was a genuine point to point without a set course, the rider with the best knowledge of the forest, who could pick the shortest route, and with the most sure-footed mount over rough ground, being the winner. For those who had come on foot or by car to Picket Post to see the riders finish there was the second spectacle of the meet of the New Forest Buckhounds.

There were few who knew the Forest better than Jack. "If I was dropped anywhere in the Forest by parachute, after five minutes I would know my way home," he declared.

To him, hunting was an integral part of forest life. The deer had to be kept down, he declared, and having so often on foot or on Percy helped to drive small herds from the fields where they were grazing the crops, I could see this point.

"Some people think that the hounds tear the buck to pieces, but they only hold it at bay while I go in with my knife. It is killed instantly. The hounds get the offal."

He believed that animals capable of such speed were born to be hunted. One evening he took down the long hunting horn from its place on the wall and invited us to test our wind. Blow as I might I could not raise a sound and handed it to Richard who raised a few staccato burps from the instrument. Then Jack blew a long, resounding note that shattered our ear drums until his wife took it away from him.

"Not indoors Jack! Tis a sight too loud," and the horn was replaced over the doorway.

At last, Jack would pull out his watch on its chain. "Time you went home, lad, and you were in bed, my lady, if you're going to be up in time for your round tomorrow."

Richard would get up then and make for the door. I had noticed of late that he paused before leaving and looked at me. I interpreted the look, but from sheer perversity I chose to ignore it. Dot, too, had noticed.

"You're very unkind to him, Jose," she reproved me as his reluctant footsteps passed the window. She was right. I was being unkind, but I could not now run after him. I could, though, by going quickly through the hall, meet him at the front door. Now very few people in the country use their front doors – in fact I had never seen the one at the kennel cottage open, but I did not expect to find it fastened with a key and two bolts that would have held Fort Knox. I first attacked the key. It would not budge. Even wrapped in my handkerchief and held with both hands it remained fast. Richard's footsteps had drawn level with the porch. He would soon reach the gate and his bike. I gave the key another hard twist. It grated and turned. Richard paused at the sound, then went on. Now for the top bolt. This proved as obstinate as the lock. Frantically I worked at it as I heard the click of the gate, then Richard taking his bike from the fence. I was determined now to get out, but still the bolt would not yield. Then suddenly it shot back with a report like the opening of a cell door. The second one was comparatively easy. Before I had got out of the door, Richard was on the porch.

One of the things a woman remembers all her life is her first kiss, the first one that really means something, like this one on the kennel cottage porch, in summer darkness, while owls screeched from the cover, hounds shifted restlessly on their platform, and Percy ripped at the grass in the paddock.

He made it last, as if it were something for which he had waited a long time.

"I've wanted to do that for ages," he said at last.

"Why didn't you?"

"You didn't exactly encourage me. I was dead scared to!"

It was odd to think of Richard being scared of anything, least of all me, but this was only one of many surprises since that first unfavourable impression, which now seemed so long ago. It was hard to imagine that he was the same person who had been so abominably rude and insisted on putting cats in my room. I said something of the sort.

"Well I had to make you notice me somehow!"

"Was it that hard?"

"It was hellish hard!" he replied ruefully. "Anyway, I liked to make you angry. You were so funny."

There followed then that 'time of enchantment' wherein 'all days are fair and all fields green'. We thought only of the present, oblivious even to the shadow of the war and impending separation; to the pervading gloom on the farm as continued bad weather wreaked havoc on the harvest. We were concerned only in spending as much time as possible in each other's company. It was not easy. Although rain still frequently stopped work in the fields, evenings and weekends were often the times when the corn was dry enough to cut, or we could get out and turn the shocks which were turning green with sprouting corn. I suggested meeting Richard from ATC when I'd finished work. He agreed and the following evening when the full harvest moon rose like a great cheese over the woods, we met on the road half way to Brockenhurst and, leaving our bikes, walked and talked under the trees in Hollands Wood, where shafts and pools of silver light lay between dark shadows. Happily we discussed the events of the day and laughed together over those comical incidents that constantly occurred on farm and milk round. Sometimes we talked of the future; a future together, however distant that might be.

"I wish this war would end so that we could get down to something sensible – like getting a farm, getting married," Richard said often. "It'll be donkey's years even after the war before I'll be able to settle down."

I said it didn't matter. I didn't want to be married for ages anyway. There were lots of things I planned to do first. After the war I wnted a job with horses, and Jack was teaching me all he could.

"Anyway," he said, "I want to have a crack at Jerry first!"

So he would take his part in the war and after that, however long it took, I would wait for him.

"They say the life expectancy of a bomber pilot is six weeks," he remarked later, in a matter-of-fact tone, as if to test my reaction. I had heard that it was somewhat less than that, but I refused to think about it – yet.

"You're spending too much time courting," Jack complained one evening. "You don't ride now. That horse needs exercise." indicating Percy as he restlessly paced the paddock fence.

"I'll get Sultan again," said Richard. "We'll go together on Sunday. Doesn't look as if we'll be harvesting. Have you ever seen the Knightwood Oak?"

"No but I'd like to."

"I'll take you."

It rained heavily on Saturday night so we were free to ride on Sunday. Richard fetched Sultan before lunch so that we could start immediately afterward.

The way lay through Queen's Bower. We followed the stream that was so clear between its sandy banks, that we could see shoals of tiny fish darting swiftly to and fro amid the reflection of the oak trees. Further on beeches replaced the oaks and the stream deepened. In places we could see where the deer came down to drink. Then we came to a ford where it ran over a smooth gravel bed and round a bend into a wide deep pool.

"This would be a good place to swim if it weren't so far," said Richard.

Eventually the path came out on the Lyndhurst-Bournemouth road and turning left we followed it through open country of gorse and heather. Under the umbrella of the woods we had not noticed heavy spots of rain. Now they were falling faster. With my usual optimism about all things, including the weather, I was not wearing a jacket, although Richard had been wiser.

"It's going to be heavy" he said. "Had we better turn back?"

"I never turn back," I replied stoically, refusing the offer of his jacket. "I'm used to getting wet."

So we went on through a rapidly increasing downpour until, where the trees again come down to the roadside, we went through a gate into the Enclosure, which I was surprised to find was full of giant conifers, but further along the wide ride between their orderly ranks was a grove of great beech trees. There, in the centre dwarfing them all, was the Knightwood Oak.

"It's supposed to be the oldest and largest oak in England," Richard told me as I sat gazing at its great girth, and blinking out the rain that stung my eyes. I thought how it must have started its life in the time of Stephen and been full grown by Elizabeth's reign.

"I'm glad I've seen it," I said.

With a last look at the forest giant we followed the soggy green ride between the beeches. There are few places wetter than the forest on a rainy day when the deluge from the skies is accentuated by dripping trees. I was now thoroughly drenched, my thin shirt clinging to me like a wet suit, my hair in rat's tails, I began to feel chilled.

"Come on, let's canter," said Richard. "Race you to the end of the ride!"

Sultan, the bigger, stronger horse, made little of the heavy going and was soon ahead, but Percy was going well and gradually caught up as we sped through the rain. Watching

Sultan as we drew level I did not see three greasy planks of wood that bridged a stream. Sultan jumped them, but Percy trod them, slipped and came crashing gown, throwing me flat on my face and stomach in a quagmire of soft mud. Utterly winded by the fall I lay still, while Percy's flailing hooves came dangerously close. Then he was up and a moment later so was I, both without injury but with a liberal coating of thick clay.

I must have looked extremely comical but there was not a vestige of a smile on Richard's face. He had dismounted and looked as shaken as Percy and I felt. "Don't look so serious," I said. "You've always joked about my falls."

"I've never seen you do it before," he answered, wiping the worst of the mud from my eyes and mouth with his handkerchief, and from Percy's saddle and bridle with some long, coarse grass.

"It was one of my more spectacular exhibitions," I told him.

"I should think so. He damn near rolled on you."

We remounted and walked on quietly, letting Percy recover, the rain serving now to clean us a little.

The Slightams were out when I got home. I washed my hair and put my clothes to soak in one bath and myself in another, grateful that the kennel cottage boasted a constant supply of hot running water. As I lay and soaked I thought that I would long remember our ride to the Knightwood Oak.

The first week in September the weather relented and allowed several fields of corn to be carried. As a change from shocking sheaves Joy and I now pitched them as we loaded the trailers and wagon along with the gypsies. I enjoyed pitching as I did any job that had a rhythm to it; stabbing the sheaf just above the string, swinging it up onto the load and turning the prong so that it pulled out easily and did not pierce the legs of the loader, and so on to the next at an easy rhythmical pace. Mrs Witcher led the horse.

"Can't expect me to do pitching - not the way I am," she said.

"I should think not, Mrs Witcher," I agreed, the 'way she was' being now quite obvious.

In September the sheep were sold and Richard and I went no more to the golf course on our free evenings. Diana, with Dee-Two left the caravan for her parents' farm near Beaulieu Road station. When Richard and I went to the annual Beaulieu Road pony sale in October we spent the afternoon with her a few weeks before Bob died.

During those halcyon days of the past summer I could not have envisaged leaving the farm. It happened quite suddenly, after my very worst morning on the round. The rain had returned with a heavy, depressing downpour, my customers had been unusually complaining, Joey had run away twice dragging his anchor, and each time leaving a trail of broken bottles to be picked up. The second time the local bobby appeared round a corner and bore down upon me. He was a veritable 'Mr Plod' – stout and ruddy of cheek with black, bushy brows and moustache.

"Look here, my girl, we can't have all this broken glass left around," he growled with mock ferocity, for he was really a jovial fellow, "You'll have to pick every bit up."

I replied that I was just about to. I wondered that he had not taken me to task about my errant pony or for exceeding the speed limit with a milk float…

"I'll hold the brute for you," he offered.

Leaving Joey in the firm hands of the law I picked up the widely scattered pieces of glass, while the rain beat down on my back and my finger bled copiously from a deep cut.

"Sorry about that" said the bobby, "Is it bad?"

I shook my head, wrapping my bleeding finger in my handkerchief and taking Joey from him. I had been on the round since 7am. It was now 1.30pm and I still had to take Joey to be shod.

"How much longer are you going to drive this pony?" asked the farrier as he pulled off Joey's shoes, for the pony's antics were well known.

"I haven't much choice" I replied.

He grunted as he threw aside the pincers and reached for the hoof parers.

"Heard of a nice little job yesterday – just suit you. Mr Foster up at Wilverley Lodge wants a girl to look after two cows and calves and help generally with his smallholding.

"I don't want to leave the farm, or the kennels," I told him. "Besides, we're not supposed to find our own jobs. We're expected to stay in the ones we're sent to."

"Well, I just hope you don't have an accident. I'll give you Mr Foster's 'phone number in case you change your mind."

I took the proffered grimy piece of paper with the figures scrawled on it, put it in my pocket and thanked him.

Joey bolted again on the way home, stopping only when we got to the dairy door. As I unloaded the milk crates I thought about the job at Wilverley. I knew the place. Richard and I had cycled by it on the way to Bournemouth when we spent the day with his parents. I remembered the Lodge and its acres of land behind a screen of conifers, the sawmill beyond, and the magnificent view. On every side rolling heathland, purple with heather merged into woodland of beech and oak, with contrasting belts of dark conifers. The only other sign of habitation, seen from the Lodge gates, was a keeper's cottage, two miles away as the crow flies, its roof just discernible among the trees. To the west rose the tall finger of Sway Tower and. across the silver line of the Solent, the Isle of Wight.

It would be a wonderful place to live and work.

Forget it, I thought. You can't quit because of one bad day. Tomorrow the sun will shine, everyone will greet you with a nice smile and Joey will behave perfectly.

In the end the decision to go or stay was not with me. The boss came out to the kitchen when I was washing up after my late lunch and told me in his gentle way that Doris was joining the Land Army and would take over my round. I was redundant. A week later I moved to Wilverley.

Horses & hounds of the New Forest Buckhounds, 1941.

CHAPTER 8

Out with the Hunt

At 6am the housekeeper, Mrs Fugett, a tall, white-haired Scotswoman whom I had met the night before, was making tea in the kitchen. She poured a cup for me but before I could drink it there was a loud knocking at the back door and a gruff voice inquired if the Land Girl was ready.

In the doorway stood a small dark man whom Mrs Fugett introduced as Harry. He was the gardener and general factotum, some of whose chores I was about to take over.

"Thought you might have got here early last evening," he said, somewhat disgruntled, "so that I could have shown you round. No time now. You'll have to get on with the milking."

Richard had cycled up to Wilverley with me and we had stopped half way to stroll in the wood opposite Hinchlea Lodge, or I might have been earlier.

"I've got the cows in for you this morning," Harry told me over his shoulder as he hurried away on short bow legs which ended in large gum boots, "but you'll have to do that yourself in future."

I followed him across the wide circular drive in front of the house to a gate, on the other side of which an acre or more of furze and heather sloped steeply down to two small pastures. A complex of looseboxes, home built of pine logs, stood on the hillside. Inside one, the two cows, Molly and Mildred, were waiting to be milked.

Mildred was a Guernsey/Jersey cross, a good cow of unusual colouring, being tortoiseshell and white with the pretty black dish-face of the Jersey breed. Molly was pure Guernsey, yellow and white. They were both quiet and gave down their milk easily.

When I'd finished milking, I took a bucketful to feed their offspring in the next box. The cows and their calves were entirely my responsibility. Harry looked after Betsy, the sow, who was so docile that she came running to his whistle and followed him about like a dog. Mr Foster looked after the hens himself. There was also Mr Foster's black hunter, Prince, and two forest ponies, Prudence and Puzzler, whom the daughters of the family rode when on leave from the FANYs. Puzzler, who was remarkably fast and keen for his twenty-one years, I had permission to ride.

"Don't you come off him," warned Harry, "or ee'll turn round and savage ee!"

I thought this unlikely, although he disliked men and had bitten Harry on occasion.

After bringing the milk up to the house there was work to do in the little dairy behind the kitchen. I skimmed the cream from the large pan of milk set the previous day, salted that which was put ready for making butter and put the skim in a pail for Betsy. Then I washed the utensils and went in to breakfast.

Mrs Fugett, with whom I had my meals, was kind but taciturn and few words passed between us as we sat at the table in the kitchen window. Harry, by contrast, was extremely garrulous, but because he was very deaf, conversation was somewhat one-sided. He was possessed of a frenzied urgency.

"Never enough time to get round everything!" he complained constantly. "So much to do I never knows which way to turn," and he would stand for five or ten minutes enumerating his tasks while I thought how many he could be doing if he were not taking the time to tell me about them.

The current job was digging the kitchen garden after the harvest of summer vegetables. Harry showed me the correct way to dig, taking a spade's depth and throwing the soil back so that a deep, clean trench was left. There was a day spent mulching the fruit bushes with manure from the midden behind the stables, and days picking apples from the orchard behind the house. Two days a week we harnessed Prudence to a small cart and drove to a farm four miles across the forest where Mr Foster had bought an acre of grass for silage. Harry cut the grass with a scythe while I used a rip hook, putting the grass into sacks which we loaded into the cart at the end of the day. We turned Prudence out in an adjoining paddock.

"Have you ever noticed," said Harry, leaning for a moment on his scythe and nodding his head toward the pony, "how horses have regler times fer grazing. Prue's had her head down since we come but you watch, at 12 o'clock sharp she'll stop."

I watched. At 12 o'clock we stopped for lunch and Prue stopped grazing.

In the afternoon Harry let me take a turn with the scythe. After brief instruction I took to the task like a duck to water and have ever since loved to use a scythe or watch its use in capable hands; the steady rhythmical movement, the blade held low to the ground and level. I can never watch it being clumsily used without wincing.

It seemed late in the year for making silage.

"Is there enough goodness in the grass now?" I asked Harry when he paused to stretch his back.

"Umm, maybe, maybe not" he answered, as if not caring much either way."Still, while we'm doin' this we'm doin' nothin' else…" which was his favourite philosophical observation when engaged on something he considered tedious or a waste of time.

The silo, measuring ten feet in diameter, was encased in sisalcraft paper and pig netting. The job of treading the silage for twenty minutes twice daily to press out the air fell to me.

The horses provided a diversion from this weekly routine when they broke out of their paddock and galloped away across Wilverley Plain. It took Harry and me most of the day to get them back, trudging over the heather, halters in our hands, our pockets bulging with sugar, carrots and cow nuts intended to persuade three errant quadrupeds who were having the time of their lives, that they would be better off at home.

I had one day off a week and I was free on Sundays apart from milking. On Sunday afternoons Richard cycled over from the farm and I recounted the experiences of my new job in exchange for news of the farm and kennels. I could not suppress a smile when he told me that the day after I left, Joey had bolted with Joe Fripp and overturned the float, throwing out churns and bottles with the redoubtable Joe himself, into the ditch. The pony had been sold immediately and Brownie brought back out of retirement until a permanent replacement could be found.

In spite of continued indifferent weather the harvest was completed on the farm by the end of September and in the park a week later. October, as if to make amends for all that had gone before, was a glorious month of golden days and silver nights. Free now from overtime Richard cycled up two or three nights a week. It was the Hunter's moon now that illuminated the open heath and shone through the aisles of tall conifers as through the lancets of a cathedral window.

Sometimes we walked to the 'Naked Man' – the old trunk of an oak, long ago struck by lightning, a jagged branch raised on either side like supplicating arms; denuded of bark it was ghostly white in the moonlight. We returned through the enclosure where conifers gave place to fine beeches and then a small larch wood. Below Wilverley Lodge, the sawmill lay in a pool of light, the big blade silent.

At the kennels preparations were in progress for the season's hunting. Percy had gone. I did not mention the fact, neither did Jack. I had known all along that it must happen sometime and I'd had six months of happy riding with him. I was sad, all the same, remembering how willing and companionable he had always been. There had been the time when I had ridden him twelve miles across the forest to Fawley to visit Felicity's mother and Mr Soffe, with a packet of sandwiches for my lunch and a nosebag for Percy tied to my saddle; and the evening I got lost and found myself, at dusk, half way to Bournemouth. Alarmed at the way cars drew up close to Percy's hindquarters in the then total darkness, I stopped at an inn and telephoned the farm and Richard cycled to meet me.

There were four horses now in the stables: Michael, Jack's own horse, black, strong and hot headed; two chestnut mares, Swallow and Rachel, and Jim's mare, called Big Bertha because she was seventeen hands and during the summer months was used for light work on his mother's farm. But clipped out, mane and tail trimmed, she passed for a handsome heavy hunter. Because she was the most manageable, I often rode Bertha alone although the contrast in our size never failed to amuse Jack.

"Did you ever see a pea on a drum?" he laughed.

Beside the work that went on in kennel, flesh-house and stables, there were extra chores for Dot as well. She often helped feed and groom the horses and cared for Jack and Jim's livery. Sometimes in the evening I watched her cleaning the brass buttons of their hunting jackets, by the light of the oil lamp, first sliding the metal guard under the buttons to protect the dark green cloth, then burnishing with a soft brush, then a duster and finally wrapping each button in tissue paper to preserve the shine. Sometimes she polished their boots, getting that final mirrorlike shine with a smooth bone.

My days off were now spent riding to exercise with the hounds and with them I discovered many new areas of the Forest. The three hours ride included many miles of road work in order to harden the hounds' pads. I was riding Swallow when we set off one morning on the main road toward Brockenhurst, and immediately met an army convoy. Swallow, I found, disliked the vehicles as much as Joey had done, and staying on her back took all my concentration.

"She'll teach you to sit down in the saddle, my lady," Jack grinned, watching the mare prance and shy. Certainly half an hour on Swallow did wonders to improve my grip!

When we reached the level crossing in the village the gates were closed and horses and hounds stood quietly while a goods train lumbered past. Then suddenly an express roared through like a rocket. Each horse whipped round and bolted in a different direction. The hounds scattered far and wide. A small crowd had gathered when we arrived, all admiring, some fondling the hounds, but when we pulled up our mounts, turned them and collected up the pack, there was not a soul to be seen, except the farrier, who stood in the doorway of his forge convulsed with laughter.

"Where did everyone go?" Jack chuckled. But even when the gates had opened and we had crossed the lines, no-one had emerged.

On my way home that day I saw Mr & Mrs Henry Witcher crossing the lawn toward the cover. As they stopped I could see that Mrs Witcher had in her arms a small grubby bundle.

"Can I see the baby, Mrs. Witcher?" I asked, getting off my bike; well knowing that was their reason for waiting. The gypsy proudly turned back the blanket from a tiny white face below a thatch of black hair.

"She's been poorly", Mrs Witcher told me, as if in explanation of the child's puny state.

"In 'orspital," added Henry gravely.

"I didn't like the way she were treated" complained the indignant mother. "Put in a bath an' washed all over. I were glad t' get 'er back and look after 'er proper."

"Well, I hope she goes on all right now," I said, although I felt less than optimistic about the poor little mite.

At Wilverley Lodge, although I seldom saw the need for Harry's panic, there was still plenty to do. The silo was finished and the late apples were gathered. I was now initiated into the task of mixing cement as Harry and I put a floor in the new calf pen that he and Mr Foster had built during the summer. I spent a morning digging wheelbarrow loads of gravel out the hillside. Cement bags were the heaviest I had ever handled, but Harry and I managed between us and mixed two of gravel to one of cement, adding water from the butt by the stable. When the new floor was dry and hard we put down some bedding and moved in the two calves. There was soon to be a third. The day that Molly vas due to calve found Harry fussing like an anxious father.

"If she ain't dropped it by tonight, means I'll have t' keep gettin' up t' watch 'er." he grumbled. He did, and the early hours found him sitting on a bale of straw in the loose box while Molly peacefully chewed the cud. She calved quickly and easily while he was at breakfast...

Throughout October I spent many hours on the hillside cutting bracken which Harry and I made into a rick for the cows' winter bedding. At the same time I cleared the gorse so that next spring there would be more grazing for them. It was a job I enjoyed, feeling like a pioneer clearing the bush, while Harry went about his own chores. One of these was a little errand with Mildred, for where there are only one or two cows with no husband of their own at home, a journey must be made to the nearest suitable bull. Harry set off after breakfast with Mildred on a halter, on a long walk to a Guernsey breeder several miles away. Getting there was uneventful, but Mildred showed every reluctance to being taken home. After a slow and difficult half mile Harry stopped to cut a stout switch. Milly chose this moment for a sharp about face and a lively canter in the direction from whence she had come; Harry desperately holding on to the rope, unable to stop her. A hot, dishevelled and angry man arrived, willy-nilly, back at the farm and insisted that a boy should accompany him and his obstreperous cow to Wilverley.

Next morning Harry was still footsore and disgruntled but Milly, standing quietly in her stall, looked as if butter wouldn't melt in her mouth.

The beautiful Indian summer stretched into November, with misty mornings, warm days and fierce crimson sunsets behind russet woods. Then about mid-month I awoke one morning to the sound of a westerly gale tearing through the trees and rain lashing against the windows. Raincoated and gumbooted I went out to fetch the cows.

"Aah, this'll set in now fer a bit," Harry observed. "It'll put an end to yer courting!"

Harry had not failed to notice how often and how long Richard's bicycle leaned against the fence.

He was right, and with the inclement weather and long dark evenings the isolation of Wilverley closed about me. I spent my days with deaf Harry and mealtimes with the silent Mrs Fugett, who, after 6.30 dinner, went to visit her sister who lived in the nearby village of Wootton. I was left alone with the Aga, a disdainful Siamese cat who acknowledged no-one but the housekeeper, and without even the diversion of a radio. Sometimes Mr Bunch, the cocker spaniel, would come out and keep me company. He was by far the most sociable animal on the place, for Zena, the wolfhound was as aloof as the Siamese. One could hold a conversation with Mr Bunch for although silent, his eyes and ears and ever wagging stumpy tail registered a whole range of responses. Then Zena came into season and Mr Bunch was banished to kennels for three weeks.

On 7th December Mrs Foster called me into the lounge with the family and Mrs Fugett to listen to the 6 o'clock news. In shocked silence we heard of the Japanese attack on Pearl

Harbour. During the following day's awareness of this new dimension of the war was uppermost in our minds. The war news did nothing to lighten my spirits, depressed by the solitude of Wilverley. What had happened, I wondered, to the girl who was so self-contained; happy with her own company. That was before I had known the richness of close companionship. I badly needed something else to do and willingly agreed when asked to help at the WVS canteen in Brockenhurst for three hours, two nights a week. Here, in company with a pleasant, elderly helper I served tea and toast and jam to army privates, returning to Wilverley at 10pm.

It was a dark December, without moon or starlight from the overcast sky. The feeble light through the regulation narrow slit in the black paper that covered my bicycle lamp, barely showed my front mudguard. One night of impenetrable blackness I had passed over the little bridge at the top of the Weirs and through the thick woods of Hinchlea beyond which the open heathland began and the road grew steeper. Breathless, I got off my bike. It was then that I heard the footsteps. They were not very close, but steady and persistent and heavier than mine. It was just a forest pony, I told myself. I listened more intently but not daring to pause. The footsteps were definitely human; a man's footsteps and getting closer. Was he a vagrant or an escaped German prisoner? My mouth was dry and every breath hurt as I struggled up the steep incline. Near the hilltop my legs gave out and I slumped on the handlebars. If I was to be raped or murdered this was it. I could go no further. Then a dark shape came alongside and a familiar voice said, "Gosh, Jo, I thought I'd never catch up with you!"

"Richard!" I gasped. "You nearly scared me to death. Why on earth didn't you call out?"

"I don't know. I was too intent on catching you. I went to the canteen after ATC but you had gone."

I was too pleased to see him to be angry. We walked to the top of the hill in silence until we had regained our breath and remounted our bikes.

"I haven't been able to see you, even on Sundays. I've had extra Home Guard duty and a heck of a lot of swotting to do," he explained.

We talked about Pearl Harbour and the American entry into the war, and his own impatience to be taking part in it.

"Doris and Joy have been giving me dancing lessons in the sitting room to the gramophone. They said I would have to be able to dance when I'm in the RAF.

"Of course," I said. "How are you getting on?"

"Fine" he replied.

It was late when we reached the lodge. By the light in her bedroom window I knew that Mrs Fugett had already gone to bed. We could not linger over saying 'Goodnight'.

"I must go in" I said.

As Richard rode away I wondered what had made him come on this cold, dark December night and when I should see him again. We exchanged letters at Christmas when Richard went home for a week, and I had Christmas Day off, spending it quietly with my Mother.

Jack had asked me to ride second horse to the meet at Bolder Wood Green on Boxing Day and after I had milked, fed the calves and completed my dairy chores I set of to the Kennels. I arrived to a scene of feverish activity. Jack was bustling with even more than his usual briskness; saddles were being slapped on and horses led out with urgent haste.

"Come on, we're late starting!" Jack called to me, while Jim handed me Swallow's bridle and threw me into the saddle with a force that almost landed me on the other side. Then he mounted Rachael and Jack got up on Michael while Marion, his niece rode Bertha, the other second horse. The hounds were let out, a seething, noisy avalanche of black and white and tan. At the sight of them Swallow ran hastily backwards until stopped by the field fence.

"Are ee comin' or goin'?" shouted Harry Witcher, who with the rest of his family had come to see us move off. Once on the road we began to trot, a brisk, relentless trot that went on mile after mile, through Lyndhurst and Minstead and deep into the forest. For me this resulted in agonising stitch.

"Lean right over your saddle," said Marion. "Touch your left toe with your right hand."

After a few moments of these gymnastics the pain eased and I enjoyed the last few miles; to be part of the hunt, to watch the eager pack with their waving white sterns and to be in a part of the forest that I had not seen before.

Due to our hasty progress we arrived at Bolder Wood punctually at 11 o'clock. Most of the field had already gathered on the wide green in front of a keeper's cottage and outbuildings. A forester came from the woods and went over to Jack.

"He's telling him where he's seen a buck harboured," said Marion.

"Harboured?" I enquired.

Marion, a keeper's daughter and bred in the Forest, stared in amazement at my ignorance. "Where he is laid up for the daytime," she explained.

The main pack were put into one of the sheds and Jack, following the man's directions, led off with the tufters, while Marion and I were left to walk our horses up and down,

"How long will they be?" I asked.

"It depends. One day last week I waited an hour-and-a-half."

But today we were lucky. In little more than twenty minutes Jack and Jim were back, hurling themselves from their sweating mounts and onto the fresh ones. The full pack were laid on and in a few moments they were riding into the forest, dark green liveries merging with lichen-covered tree trunks, chestnut mounts with russet bracken and beech leaves. As the baying of hounds and the notes of Jack's horn faded into the distance, in a strange stillness, Marion and I mounted, and turning our horses' heads toward home, walked them quietly back along the roads where we had trotted so vigorously an hour before.

To my delight I was riding Rachael.

"She's the most beautiful mare I've ever seen," I once said to Jack.

"Aah, she's a beauty to ride too," he replied, "She's velvet."

"Jack treasures that mare like gold," said Dot. "I doubt he'll let you ride her." But he had done, if only into Brockenhurst to the farrier, with Jim riding Michael and leading Swallow.

On the way home we had cantered across the greens behind the village and I knew what Jack meant when he said she was 'velvet'. In a long, smooth stride her feet seemed hardly to touch the ground. Even today, all the way at a walk, she held her head so beautifully and trod so daintily she was a joy to ride.

Back at the kennels, after we had stabled our mounts, rubbed them down, put on their rugs and filled their hay nets, we ate our sandwiches and I cycled back to Wilverley in time to milk the cows again.

"We are all going to a dance and social tonight at the village hall," Dot had said as I left the Kennels. "Come back when you've finished work and come with us."

So I did, returning to Wilverley about midnight, having cycled sixteen miles, ridden fourteen, walked a few more and danced for several hours. It had been quite a day.

The last days of December brought a grey, relentless cold and a frost which turned the ground to iron and every outside source of water to solid ice. We kept the cows in; their boxes well bedded with bracken we had harvested in the autumn. Nestling up to their warm flanks at milking time in this cosy shelter was a welcome respite from outside work. Then, on the first day of the New Year, as I carried the afternoon milk to the dairy, a few large feathery flakes of snow drifted gently from the leaden sky, hesitatingly, like white clad ballerinas uncertain of their cue. Next morning heavy snow bowed the branches of the conifers and levelled the open forest to one white trackless waste. Harry and I took shovels and dug our way to the loose boxes to milk the cows and feed the hunter, then struggled to the field with hay for the ponies which preferred to live out whatever the weather. Feeding now became the principal task of the day. We had tapped the silo early in December and Mildred and Molly had found it palatable. Mr Foster bought a load of kale and daily I put some of this mixed with straw through an ancient chaff cutter housed in a lean-to shed at the end of the stables. It snowed on three consecutive Tuesdays and in between bitter winds whipped the white blanket to the consistency of cake icing and turned the roads to ice. Ponies and deer barely dinted the smooth surface and the smaller animals' tracks were invisible.

After nearly three weeks of being snowed up we awoke one morning to the sound of dripping eaves and running water and a wind blowing softly from the south. Now it was February and the first harbingers of spring appeared in the woods and in the garden; the spiky yellow blossom of the witch hazel, glistening clumps of snowdrops, celandines and hazel catkins. One afternoon I saddled Puzzler and rode along the soggy Forest paths for the first time since December.

About this time I met two girls from the Timber Corps who were working temporarily at the sawmill; Yvonne, who was very pretty with wide, grey eyes and short brown curls, and Christine who was tall and elegant. One evening they showed me round the mill with its sheds full of long planks, piles of sawdust and huge tree trunks awaiting that great, wicked toothed blade that whirled with such terrifying speed. How easily it could sever a wrist or a limb.

"Some of the girls operate those things" Yvonne told me with a shudder. "There are men who won't take on the job, but the Timber Corps do it."

This section of the WLA was newly formed. In time it numbered 4,000 and these Lumber Jills did every job in the forest from measuring trees to felling. Yvonne and Christine had just come from Wales where they had been 'pole selecting'.

"We walked miles and miles every day through the trees and then miles home at night to our billets. Some were pretty quaint, too." I noticed that their badges differed from mine, having a conifer tree as its emblem instead of a wheatsheaf. The girls had become friendly with two young subalterns stationed near Burley. They found a companion for me, their Quartermaster, known to us all as Q. He was rather old, I thought, probably forty, but he was jovial and amusing. The six of us went to several local dances during the next few weeks and life became brighter. Then the girls were sent to the Forest of Dean and I was alone again.

The following Sunday, Land Girls from the area took part in a parade of all the Services at Lymington. We were taken there by coach and arrived at a playing field already crowded with youth in uniform. We formed ranks between the St John's Ambulance Brigade and the Territorials. After a short ceremony we all moved off to parade through the streets of Lymington. Unlike the other services, we were unused to marching on parade. Some of us walked miles a day behind a horse, others delivering milk, through fields pushing a hoe or along lanes to fetch the cows, but march we did not! All the same, I do not think we disgraced ourselves when, after all the clipped, resounding commands, the heel clicking and the drilled precision of the Army and the Air Force both male and female, our representative turned to us and called gently, "Come along girls."

I thought that Richard must be somewhere in that throng with the ATC. I had not seen him since December. One evening in a fit of loneliness I had telephoned him from a call box when I had finished my stint at the canteen. He had been offhand, even curt, as if annoyed that I had done so, and I remembered reading somewhere that the tragic thing about young love was the misguided belief that it would never end. I knew that with Richard and me it was going to end. It happened one Sunday morning when I met him by chance at the kennels. We walked in a strained silence from the tack room where we had been talking to Jack. Suddenly he kicked viciously at a stone, dug his hands deeper into his pockets and muttered, without looking at me.

"Jo, all that talk about marriage … its no good. It'll be years before I get a farm, even after the war. We'd better forget about it."

As I thought, he felt himself entrapped. Well, I knew when to let go."

"That"s all right," I said lightly, "I never took you that seriously anyway."

"Oh, I thought you did."

"It was fun talking about it, but its no good taking anyone seriously in wartime is it?"

Dreams woven in moonlit woods on summer nights seldom withstood the winter chill of separation and uncertainty.

"We could still be friends and perhaps see each other occasionally," he said, but with a lack of enthusiasm that discouraged any positive response I might have made.

It was better, I said, to call it a day. Better nothing at all, than just a casual friendship when, just a short time ago we had been so close. We had reached the end of the drive and I took my bicycle from the fence. Then I wished him luck and said "Goodbye."

Perhaps nothing hurts so much at the time because one never really believes that it is happening. It was in the weeks that followed that the sense of utter desolation hit me.

"Did you have to break it off so completely?" Dot asked me.

"I don't know. Maybe I was wrong. Anyway, it's done now."

"Oh well, few girls marry the first man they fall in love with. You'll get over it."

No doubt I would, eventually. Meanwhile, there would be a poignant Richard-shaped gap in my life.

Shortly after this I had a letter from Diana, who was now an Admin. Officer in the WAAF and enjoying every minute.

'If you get tired of the Land Army Jo,' she wrote, 'Join the WAAF – it's a great life.'

I was unlikely to tire of the Land Army but I had grown restless at Wilverley. I wanted to do more for the war effort by working on a farm again, helping to produce food for the country rather than for one family. I got in touch with the understanding Mrs Brown and she arranged a move for me to a four hundred acre farm near Portsmouth.

Just before I left, I wrote to Richard, telling him about my new job and giving him the address of my billet should he feel like writing to me when he was in the RAF, but he did not reply.

Soon afterwards I heard that he was in South Africa starting his pilot's training. He would soon have his 'crack at Jerry'.

As for me, it was time to move on.

CHAPTER 9

Tin Lizzie

The train lurched to a halt at Fareham station. A Naval rating, travelling with his companions to Gosport, got up and handed down my case from the rack. In the station yard, a tall man in corduroys and a tweed jacket waited beside an ancient Bedford lorry from which the rust and farm mud had obliterated almost all evidence of its original maroon colour.

"Mr Houghton?" I enquired.

He turned and smiled. He was quite young, his fresh complexion and clear blue eyes giving him boyish appearance.

"You'll be Josephine. Hop up," he said, indicating the high rickety cab, while he slung my case and bicycle into the back of the lorry on top of some potato sacks. Mounting the step I found the passenger seat already occupied by a determined looking Jack Russell terrier bitch, which stared at me balefully as if daring me to move her.

"Shift over, Midge" her master commanded.

Midge inched grudgingly across the seat and I slid cautiously onto the remaining space. Mr Houghton got out the starting handle and cranked the engine. After a few false starts it roared into a convulsive vibration that caused my teeth to chatter and Midge to shake like a white blancmange. The farmer climbed up, and after a noisy selection of gears, steered the shuddering vehicle into the traffic.

Once out of the town we started to climb, the old lorry sweating and puffing up the steep road that led onto Ports Down, guarded by its line of red brick forts. Below us lay the flat, built-up area that fringed Southampton Water.

We discussed that never-failing topic of conversation of especial interest to the farmer, the weather; the effect upon the land of the January snow and the wet February.

"It's made us very behind with the spring ploughing for the roots. That's what you'll be doing mostly for a bit. You can plough?" he raised an inquiring eyebrow.

"No, I've never done any," I confessed.

"Hmm, thought you had. Oh well, we'll just have to teach you."

As Fort Southwick came into view on the brow of the hill and we could see Portchester Castle below, we turned away from the coast down a steep, narrow lane.

"Those are my arable fields," said the farmer, waving his hand toward both sides of the road. "I've about four hundred acres."

The country looked barren, I thought, after the Forest, with fences instead of hedges and trees dividing the fields, but as we descended I saw a small oak and hazel wood and a line of elms by the field edge. Opposite these we turned into a farm track, hemmed on one side by a high flint wall over which reared the tall gables and chimneys of the farmhouse. The buildings consisted of the usual stables, cart shed and calf pens and a large barn, while a second capacious building contained the cow stalls and dairy. A spring that rose in the middle of the sloping yard flowed down to water meadows where the dairy herd and dry stock grazed.

"Now you've seen the farm I'll take you to your billet," said Mr Houghton. Half way up the main street of the village he stopped the lorry by a thatched, clap boarded cottage standing high on a bank, and carried my bike and case up the steep slope, through the garden gate to the back door, where a tiny, elderly woman was waiting. She was Mrs Coleby, he said, who would look after me. Then with "See you at 7am tomorrow," he strode away and moments later I heard renewed protests from the Bedford as she chugged and rattled her way through the village.

"You can put your bike in the shed, then take your case upstairs. You room's on the right," Mrs Coleby told me. Her tone was curt and abrupt. Looking at her I felt a vague uneasiness. Though small and birdlike as a robin there was something of the eagle in the fierce, direct gaze of her large hooded green eyes. Her long thick waving hair which must once have been rich chestnut still retained some of its former colour. Her mouth, although set in tight lines, had once been shapely and I thought she could easily have been, in her youth, the village beauty.

"Well, go on up." she said tartly.

There were but two rooms at the top of the steep, narrow flight of stairs. Mine had adequate floor space but the ceiling, sloping sharply on either side, allowed little room to stand upright. Most of this was taken up by a large brass bedstead. By the tiny window under the thatch was a washstand which also served as a dressing table, and hanging on the door, a long red cotton bag which was my wardrobe. As such it left much to be desired. Inevitably when I hung up one garment others would fall to the bottom of the bag, and reaching into its depths was fraught with difficulty.

Having unpacked, I ran downstairs, not noticing the heavy low beam over the doorway at the bottom until I had almost knocked myself out against it.

"Ha, you'll learn to look out for that!" observed Mrs Coleby without sympathy.

At that moment the latch lifted and a tall man, bending low, having long ago gained a respect, as I had just done, for low lintels, came into the kitchen. His lean, lined face was russet brown, his hair and moustache snowy white, and his expression, like his voice, was as gentle as his wife's was sharp. Mr Coleby's entrance was a signal to make the tea from the big iron kettle that had been boiling for some time on the hob. Tea was a sparse meal and never varied. It consisted of two slices of bread and margarine, without jam, and put on my plate to indicate my ration, and one slice of cake. This was home made and nicely baked. When, at the end of each week, it was gone Mrs Coleby made another one, identical to the last and always appearing on the table upside down, because, she said, it "fitted the plate better that way". After tea I said I would like to explore the village.

"You won't find much to explore, my dear" said Mr Coleby, "But 'tis quite pretty, what there is."

There were in fact, just two streets, one crossing the top of the other like the letter T. A little Norman church with its square belfry stood at the junction, ancient cottages lining the road on either side, except where the red brick wall of the park reached down to The Red Lion. At the other end, facing the church, was the vicarage and a few larger houses. The spring dusk fell early and I returned to my billet as Mrs Coleby was lighting the oil lamp. The three of us sat round it, Mr Coleby in his wheelback carver chair, Mrs Coleby and I on upright kitchen chairs more conducive to a straight back than to comfort.

I was back to the primitive living: lamplight, a zinc bath filled with hot water from the copper, and that little hut at the bottom of the garden where the chill March wind whistled through the cracks and under the door. At 7 o'clock Mrs Coleby rose to get the supper of bread and cheese and apples, and cups of cocoa.

Having finished our apples we each solemnly got up and gave the pips to the budgerigar in his cage by the window. We were eating the russets, the last of the 'keepers' which had been stored all winter in the cupboards of the unused parlour. The cidery fragrance still lingered although most of the apples had gone.

My hopes of a cooked breakfast were dashed next morning when Mrs Coleby put before me a single Shredded Wheat and the set two slices of bread and margarine. I was very hungry, but I doubted that I would have fared any better than Oliver Twist had I asked for more.

Just before 7am on the farm, I joined the small arable staff in the cart shed to receive the orders for the day. Mr Houghton, with the help of Dorothy, another Land Girl, milked the herd of thirty five Friesians. Doyen of this staff at the age of 74 was Will, one of the old school of farm workers of whom there are few left and may never be any more. He had a fund of wisdom, a knowledge of country lore and a conscientious approach to the task in hand. Although his back and limbs were bent with years of heavy work his keen blue eyes were as clear as a boy's. He walked from his cottage at the very top of the village but was always the first to arrive in the morning, carrying in a rush bag his dinner of bread and cheese and a raw onion and something brown in a bottle which I had supposed to be beer until Will, with a chuckle, corrected me.

"Thought it was pretty flat beer, didn't you, m'dear? That's cold tea with no milk or sugar. Most refreshing drink there is!"

There was Maurice, the Carter, who worked the two Shire horses, and Bill, the first tractor driver, a broad-shouldered, stocky man in his middle thirties. Bill was of an unpredictable temperament, sometimes jovial, sometimes surly. He seemed particularly put out, that first morning, at having to instruct me in the art of ploughing.

"Was told you knew how to plough," he grunted. I wondered how this misapprehension had arisen. "Seems I've got to teach you."

But first I had to start my tractor. Bill's was a fairly recent model, but mine could have been Fordson's prototype. I immediately named her Tin Lizzie. Starting her in the morning was one of the major tasks of the day. Mere cranking of the engine was not enough; a lot of swinging of the starting handle was involved. On cold mornings the engine was so stiff that I was unable to move it until Bill found me a four foot length of iron piping, which, attached to the handle, gave me greater leverage. Condensation of the plugs was one reason for Lizzie's morning reluctance. To remedy this Bill took out his own tractor plugs, putting mine in their place and running the engine until they were hot, then returning them to Lizzie. This switch had sometimes to be done several times before she spluttered into life. Having once got her going I was very careful not to stall or stop her until dinner time.

"Hitch on your plough," instructed Bill brusquely, when we reached the field. Then he showed me how to set it; the correct depth for the soil and at an angle so that the rubbish was buried but the soil did not fall right over. As it was second time ploughing there was little to bury.

"Now, if you begin straight and keep your tractor wheel in my furrow and keep the furrow wheel running straight, you can't go wrong," he said.

But I could.

"Call that straight!" Bill snorted after my first turn of the field. My attempt to mark out a new ream, aiming carefully at the guide stick at the end of the field was a complete disaster.

"Like a donkey's bloody hind leg!" was Bill's caustic comment.

I could only get better.

Mr Houghton, believing in the old adage "the Master's foot is the best dung," inspected our work several times a day, striding across the field, the diminutive Midge close to heel. After a week he conceded with cautious optimism that they "might make a ploughman of me yet."

I was more familiar with the next job, which was going over ploughed ground with the disc harrows. As I watched the blades break up the solid furrow, like knives crumbling cake, I thought nostalgically of the first time I used the discs at the farm in the forest, with Bray running up and down beside my tractor. On many mornings the furrows were covered with a dew studded gossamer film of spider web and I would sit for a moment watching it sparkle in the early sunlight, loath to destroy with my clumsy harrows the delicate work of those dawn spinners.

From October to the end of March there was always the job of potato bagging to occupy us on wet days.

At the end of the year the big barn was stacked to the rafters with newly harvested potatoes; now in spring there were the few speared remains. Will, Bill and I worked together; one loading potatoes into the riddler with the broad fork with studded prongs, another operating this machine which sorted them into firsts, seconds and seed, while the third picked out the rotten spuds, pulled off the spears and tied up the sacks. When we had got out a ton we loaded the bags into the old Bedford and Mr Houghton drove with them into Portsmouth, returning in about an hour for the next load. When Maurice joined us I was given the tedious job of mending sacks, a job that no longer exists in this day of plastic bags; the sack needle is as much an agricultural museum piece as the hay knife and the threshing drum.

Another interruption in the urgent business of field work was the arrival of the threshing tackle for the last time that winter. Threshing was probably the most unpopular job on the farm. It was hard and dirty work which, once begun, was carried through with a frantic urgency before the weather changed. With sinking hearts we heard, at the end of an afternoon, the sound of the traction engine chugging up the hill, followed by the rattle of the threshing box and trundling elevator. Once the thatch was off the roof next morning Midge was the first up the ladder, climbing comically with her short front legs bent over the rungs and her hind paws balancing skilfully on the ones below. Once up there she stayed all the morning, revelling in an orgy of mousing, swallowing adult mice and nests of young whole, and bringing them up again at intervals in little piles at our feet.

When a mouse ran up a leg of my dungarees I managed to kill it before it reached above my thigh.

"You wnts to tie a bit of binder twine tight above the knee, like I does," Wil told me, "That'll stop' em!"

Sometimes I helped Will and Bill on the rick, feeding the ever hungry mouth of the drum, but more often I worked in a cloud of black dust raking away the cavings (rubbish) at the rear of the machine. Here Maurice stood tying the sacks as they filled and wheeling them away to be loaded onto trailer and cart. It was with a sigh of relief at the end of the second day that we saw the tackle packed up and disappearing out of our sight until next winter.

Spring was now well advanced. The rooks in the high elms at the bottom of the hill had finished their nest building which had caused such a noisy altercation in the past weeks. I now knew the difference between the rook and the carrion crow. It was the crow that flapped his solitary way across the fields, while the rook was gregarious. As one old countryman so succinctly put it: "If ee sees one rook, then him's a crow. But ef ee sees a lot of crows, then them's rooks!"

In the fields, the lapwings had laid their eggs in a scrape on the bare ground. Bill and I moved them carefully out of the path of our tractors, replacing them after we had passed, while the agitated parents wheeled and screamed overhead. House Martins nested in the eaves under the thatch outside my bedroom window as they had done on the other farm. In spite of a persistent yen for the Forest, I had to concede that the country here had a quiet prettiness in its spring dress. There were flower-fringed lanes I cycled along, and primrose woods to walk in during the lengthening evenings.

Sometimes I met Bill exercising his black Labrador. There was an empathy between man and dog that revealed a gentler side to his nature as did his knowledge and care for the flowers and wildlife of the woods. Mostly now my life was a solitary affair with long hours alone on my tractor and long, lonely evenings, and I thought longingly of the company and camaraderie of last spring and summer. I saw very little of my fellow Land Girl. Not only did our work lay in different areas but Dorothy was a home-loving girl, either integrated in the domestic life of the farmhouse or visiting her family in Portsmouth. But we did share an interest in reading *The Land Girl* and followed the activities of our fellow members each month. Early in the year the WLA had presented a Typhoon to the RAF. There was a photograph of the aircraft with the name *Land Girl* and the WLA badge on its side, with its pilot. Girls had also raised money for the Red Cross. We were surprised, not having come in contact with any ourselves, at the number of leisure interests in the Land Army, not least that in West Sussex their cricket team had beaten the ATS on the County ground at Horsham. Then, in April Dorothy and I received an invitation to join a club, organised by two area representatives, that met weekly in Hambledon about five miles away. Accordingly we set off one evening after tea. The cycle ride along country lanes, green verged, with primroses clustered in the hedgerows between fields gold-tinged in the mellow evening light, eventually led us to a little hut in the centre of Hambledon village. Here, five other girls were gathered; four from a large arable farm a few miles away and another from a dairy farm in the village. We passed a pleasant hour just talking over tea and biscuits, for which we paid 1 shilling. But the club was short-lived. As the season advanced and the pressure of work grew, the girls from the big farm dozed off from sheer weariness at the meetings, or failed to turn up at all. Soon overtime forbade it altogether.

April was the month for planting potatoes, which was done with a ridge plough, consisting of two steel tapering moulds. The potatoes were dropped by hand into the furrow and at the next turn the ridges would be split apart by the plough, covering the seed and earthing it up in one operation. During potato planting, four Land Girls were engaged from a hostel some miles away. They arrived at 8.30 in a minibus and were collected at 5pm. I would not have liked, I thought, to be attached to a hostel, preferring the responsibility and continuity of being part of the working team of one farm, rather than moving always to strange ones engaged on monotonous gang jobs.

Of all the months of the year May is the most lush and fragrant, when the clotted cream of Hawthorn blossom and Elderflowers deck the hedgerows; the woods are a sweet smelling haze of bluebells and the winter corn is emerald green against the more tender shade of the hazel woods and beech trees. Will and I turned out the calves from their pens to receive their first sight and taste of fresh grass, then leaned on the fence to watch their antics as they gambolled away like an infant school children let out to play.

"You can plant your runner beans now," said Will on the 14th of the month. I had no plans to plant beans, but it was nice to know that I was free to do so.

"May 14th was always Wickham Fair Day before the War," he went on, "and that was the day to plant runner beans."

"I don't hold with that idea," replied Bill, who was inclined to be argumentative. "Mine are up six inches already."

"Then you're dang lucky not to have got 'em frosted!" Will declared.

Several days were spent cutting thistles in the wheat, and many more clearing the field by the Fort of couch. After the ground had been twice ploughed, then cultivated and chain harrowed, dried bunches of grass and roots lay on top of the clean soil ready to be raked into heaps and burned. It blazed merrily, the acrid black smoke drifting across the Down. It was interesting to work on top of the hill and see the panorama of the valley spreading into the distance; a patchwork of fields and woods broken by farms and cottages and the grey winding snakes of roads. One curious sight was a small biplane that flew along the valley, so low that from our higher altitude we looked down upon it. There were still aerial dogfights to watch over Portchester Harbour and sometimes a sudden flare of saffron and scarlet would mark the end of a barrage balloon.

Once summer gets under way the routine of the season passes quickly, and soon we were into haymaking. One June morning, Bill cut twenty acres of rye grass and trefoil. The process of carrying it was very different from the horse and wagon method I had known in the Forest. I made the acquaintance of a hay sweep, which resembled an enormous wooden comb with tines about six feet long, attached to a horizontal bar, a little wider than the front of the tractor. I drove this into the lines of hay, sweeping a great load to the foot of the elevator. I enjoyed this job, but often I had the heavier task of loading the elevator with a pitch fork amid the dust and flying seeds and bits of clover. Meanwhile the corn was ripening, and above the barley the unpleasing heads of wild oats appeared. Until now, the only type of wild oat I had ever heard of were those sown in the gay abandonment of youth. My second guess when told that we were going to pull wild oats was that they were self sown oats from a previous year's crop. Then it was explained to me that the wild oat is a weed, or type of wild grass, *Avena fatua* to be precise, and after we had spent several hours wading through the tall corn until we had pulled every one, I could well understand its unpopularity.

"Let's have a break," said Will at last, leaning against the gate at the end of the field and taking out his pipe. I watched him carefully filling and lighting it, while making the most of the few minutes rest. The day was warm and still. Although the weather had not compared with the prolonged heat of 1940 there had been plenty of sun and fine days. The oats on the hill looked golden and almost ready to cut. Idly, Will picked a little daisy-like flower and twirled it in his gnarled fingers.

"Camomile," he said with a smile. "I mind my mother making camomile tea – nettle tea, too – that were all the medicine we ever had when we were young – and I've not had much else since."

I looked at his clear pink skin, the bright eyes and the sheen on his white hair and moustache. They were indications of a life of good health and a recommendation for natural medicines.

Threshing machine, 1942.

CHAPTER 10

Harvest Time

The oats were cut the third week in July. The straw was long and the ears heavy and carrying the shoulder-high sheaves up the steep slope made shocking unusually hard work. I watched hopefully for Will to pause for his customary smoke. While we rested I looked down across the turning wheat to the fields where the wind rippled the purple heads of the barley. Barley was the most uncomfortable crop to handle. Its bristly awns scratched the hands and arms and sticking through the cellulose cotton of my shirt made an abrasive collar, which, after hours of pitching rubbed my neck completely raw.

"Now you sees why we wears a handkerchief inside our shirt" said Will. "You'd best do the same, m' dear."

To add to our small work force during harvest came the same four Land Girls who had helped with the potato planting. One of them, Daphne, never failed to amaze me. Slender, with silky ash blonde hair and soft, pale skin, she looked as out of place on a farm as Dresden china. She arrived every morning looking immaculate and stayed that way throughout the hottest, hardest day. She worked quite well, but had such a horror of almost everything that crawled or flew that I wondered why she had chosen an outdoor life.

Sometimes, in the evenings, we received some enthusiastic if unskillful assistance from the soldiers at Fort Widley. They made heavy work of pitching sheaves, using too much strength but not the knack and rhythm that makes this, like some other farm tasks, comparatively effortless. They considered that I must be some sort of Amazon to pitch for so many hours without tiring. Usually there was a loader and two to four pitchers to each trailer. I both pitched and drove Lizzie, getting up and down to move her on every ten yards or so. To have someone just sitting on the tractor driving it on at intervals was an almost unheard of luxury. At 7 o'clock on the mornings when there was no dew, while Will and Bill uncovered the rick, I got in a trailer load by myself, being pitcher, loader and driver by turns and I enjoyed this, taking pride in achieving a neat, symmetrical, if not large load, before the Land Girls arrived and Mr Houghton and Dorothy joined us after milking.

One morning, I was placing the last few sheaves in the centre when six sailors ran down the hill from Fort Southwick, heading for my trailer.

"We'll give you a hand!" they cried, having seized pitchforks on the way. In spite of my repeated protests that my load was big enough already they sent sheaves hurtling up like missiles from pitchforks turned point outward, so that I was in constant danger of being pierced through the leg.

"That's enough! No more, PLEASE!" I yelled, but still the barrage of sheaves came, until my former tidy structure was lost in the bulging mass, untidy as a rook's nest. At last they gave up and stood grinning at my precarious progress to the rick. Miraculously, I arrived there with the load intact.

When we had finished the barley Mr Houghton decided to take another cut off the clover, but before it was ricked Bill was already in the first field of wheat with the binder. I rode the machine by day and pitched hay onto the elevator in the evenings, working from early morning until dusk, then home to supper and sleep. I was happiest when working all the time and there were no empty leisure hours.

The importance of the harvest and the state of the crops superseded even the war news. The pressure of work was unrelenting and the binder was kept going from the time the dew was off the corn until it fell again, Mr Houghton and Dorothy and sometimes Mrs Houghton taking over from Bill and me at mealtimes. When we all stopped work for fifteen minutes at teatime Mrs Houghton brought out two large billy cans of tea and we sat in the shade of the rick leaning against its rough but cool side while we ate and drank and rested. One day, as I got up, Bill gave a shout. "S'truth, look at your back!" he exclaimed. I glanced quickly over my shoulder. My shirt was brown with fleas. "They won't hurt," he told me complacently. "They're not like dog or human fleas – just harvest fleas. They live in the corn."

"Never mind their habits, get them off me!" I cried. Bill grinned and getting up without too much hurry, brushed off the creatures with his hat. In future I sat a careful distance from the rick.

With tractors running continuously, the fuel was getting low in the tank and it was uncertain when we would get a fresh delivery. The boss said we could no longer keep the engines running while we unloaded at the rick. I heard this with dismay, for Lizzie was almost as difficult to start when overheated as she was from cold.

After pitching up a load and pitching it off again at the rick, having to swing the starting handle for several minutes was exhausting and exasperating, especially when Bill, waiting with his load, merely leaned against his tractor and watched me. Sometimes the boss and I got a load with the old Bedford. He pitched while I drove. It was a curious experience, steering by faith and stopping by chance. When driving her down the steep, narrow hill I said a brief but earnest prayer that I would meet nothing coming up. But the most frightening thing that happened to me on the hill was when leading Captain with a loaded cart. Although I had placed the iron slipper, which acted as a brake, under the wheel, we were less than half way down when I knew the old horse was having difficulty in holding back the load. There was fright in his eyes; he snorted and blew and leaned bank in the breeching as he tried to get a grip on the smooth slope. Talking to him softly, trying to calm him, I held his head high and leaned my own weight against the near shaft.

There was still the steepest part of the hill to go before I could turn him off the road onto the level farm track. I put from my mind the thought of what would happen in that narrow lane if he failed to make it. I kept talking to him, as gradually, with slipping feet, he inched down the steep gradient, until at last I turned him carefully into the farm. We stood, then, breathless and relieved, my face pressed to his neck while we rested. Never again did I bring him down the hill with a full load.

The weather held and by the second week in September the last sheaf was carted and the ricks stood tall and proud in the fields of cleared stubble. Although we were glad that it was all over for another year, there was an emptiness, almost a sadness about the scene, perhaps because the end of harvest was the end of summer.

❖ ❖ ❖

"Never let a man know you're tough", Mrs Slightam once said to me, "or he'll treat you like a cart mare." Although I appreciated the value of this advice I did not often take it; consequently I sometimes found myself trying to cope single handed with a job that no self-respecting man would do without help. That is how I came to be on top of Portsdown, one morning after harvest, attempting to bring down a bunch of heifers from a pasture where they had been for some weeks, to a fresh one near the farm.

"You'll be all right. They'll come quietly," the boss assured me. Now he may have told *me* that, but he failed to mention it to the heifers, and it soon became obvious that they had no intention of coming quietly, in fact, they had little intention of coming at all.

"Just open the gate and call them," the boss had said. The gate opened, I called "COME-on! COME-on!" in my best cowgirl voice, which attracted a great deal of attention and response from numerous passing soldiers and sailors, both in lorries and on foot, but absolutely none from the heifers, who were in the far corner of the field with their back ends towards me. I walked slowly over to them, repeating my call. One or two looked round in a desultory fashion and went on grazing. They ignored me with bovine scorn when I told them that there was much better grass where I wanted them to go. Eventually I got behind them and tried "GO-on!" for a change. They milled around a bit but remained more or less where they were. 'Concentrate on getting one or two moving in the right direction,' I thought, 'and the rest will follow.' This seemed to work after a while and when they saw the open gate and the big wide world outside their field there was no stopping them. But instead of taking the grassy track beside the Fort that led to the farm, they turned left and set off at a relentless trot along the main road. However, help was at hand, or so it seemed, in a group of khaki-clad onlookers.

"All right love, we'll stop them!" they shouted, as they formed an impressive line across the road. At this threat to their freedom the heifers bucked, tossed their heads and charged. This was too much for the Army. My brave Maginot Line disintegrated, scattered and ran. I hoped that they would show more resistance in the face of the enemy. On went my little bunch like Derby runners up the home straight. Given twenty minutes and a clear road they would be in Fareham. It would have taken an Olympic sprinter to have overtaken and turned them. I just managed to keep them in sight. About thirty yards ahead and to the right was the road that led down to the farm. There was small chance that they would take it. Then, to my intense relief I saw Bill's stalwart figure, arms upraised, standing at the junction. The heifers saw him too and stopped dead, like schoolgirls caught in the act of truancy and uncertain which way to turn.

"Now bring them on slowly!" Bill called.

Carefully, I eased them forward and together we turned them down the hill. At the gate of the field where they were to go Will stood waiting to direct them.

"Don't know how he expected you to bring the buggers down by yourself," said Bill. "Darn stupid I call it!" For once I was in complete agreement with him.

We were now into the 'season of mists and mellow fruitfulness'. In what remained of the light after tea I picked the last of the blackberries in the lane for Mrs Coleby to make jelly. Later Mr Coleby gathered the Coxs and Russets and stored them away in the big chest in the parlour. There had been apples from the garden all summer. First the Codlings from the gnarled tree that shaded an old seat by the bank door, then the rosy Beauty of Bath, Discoveries and Sturmers.

"Take what you like," Mr Coleby had said. "There's more than we can eat." So apples had made a welcome supplement to my sparse diet.

I found the inadequate meals, which resulted in constant hunger, the most difficult aspect of my present life to come to terms with. Mrs Coleby cooked our combined meat ration, in the form of a joint every Sunday. With homegrown vegetables it was good enough, but it was eked out in thin slices, warmed up with left over vegetables and thin gravy until midweek. After that, my main meal consisted of a piece of cheese and a few boiled potatoes. To my tentative suggestion that a cheese omelette or pudding would be a nice change, she replied with scorn that she "never could abide messes" and the subject was closed. Puddings were invariably a watery tapioca or an unpalatable concoction of cornflakes, milk and water heated in the oven.

The hours from the time the pangs of hunger became acute to the next meal seemed endless. Even so, when I lost my watch in the ploughed field, (it was returned to me, unharmed, by the harrows weeks later) I had difficulty, when working alone, in judging the time. If I looked across at the right moment to the opposite hillside, a red bus, moving slowly across the landscape would tell me it was 12 o'clock. If not, I often overshot my dinner hour.

"Doesn't your stomach tell you the times gel?" asked Will.

"My stomach," I replied, "is always a couple of hours fast!"

Will was thatching the ricks. I asked the boss if I might help him as I wanted to try my hand at the job, but he said that carrying the bundles of straw up a ladder was too heavy a job for a girl. This, in view of the work I had done, I thought was foolish. Some girls were full-time thatchers. This job, however, with hedging and ditching, remained the only ones of which I had no experience.

The first of the autumn jobs, beside ploughing, was the potato harvest and Daphne and the three other Land Girls came once more to pick up. My job with the tractor was pulling the 'spinner'. This machine consisted of four revolving prongs attached to a horizontal bar which was lowered into the ground and lifted at the end of the turn by means of a long lever. It was important to drive at just the right speed, for if too slow the prongs did not uncover the potatoes, or if too fast it would throw them over too wide an area. Either fault would bring strong protests from the pickers, who, especially after rain, were not too happy with their job anyway.

"I never could abide taterin'" declared Bill, which expressed the sentiments of us all. I wondered if Daphne would get dirty at this task, but except for a little mud on her gloves, she looked as immaculate as ever. Bill and Maurice took the loaded cart and trailer to the barn, which, by means of an elevator, was stacked to the roof once more with newly harvested potatoes.

I was pulling mangolds all day on my 21st birthday in November. While the men used their penknives to top and tail the roots, I somewhere found a butcher's knife.

"You'll take your fingers off with that," Bill warned me. But I acquired a knack whereby, as I cut off the mangold top, with the flick of the long blade I could toss it a considerable distance onto the heap. Seeing how far I could send it whizzing through the air became a sort of game which relieved the tedium of the task. As it was my birthday Mrs Houghton invited me to supper. The boss had just killed a pig and for days the farm kitchen had been a hive of activity with the making of brawn, sausages and black pudding. Before supper Dorothy and I went into Portchester on a small errand for Mrs Houghton.

It was a night of such impenetrable blackness that we could not even see the hedgerows each side of the narrow lane. Our footsteps and voices seemed so loud that we began to talk in hushed tones as if awed by the darkness. We felt, but could not see the ground level out as we approached the cross roads at the top of the hill. It was here that two forms leapt out in front of us.

"Who goes there!" bellowed a voice in our ears, while two fixed bayonets were pointed at our chests.

"We... We're Land Girls," we squeaked, edging away from the cold steel.

"Sorry girls!" The blackened faces of two very young marines peered into ours. "We're on manoeuvres. We had to challenge you."

"Well, we'll be back again in about twenty minutes," Dorothy said, "so please don't do it again." They were waiting for us when we returned and insisted on walking down the hill with us in case we were stopped by other marines.

"Will you come in for some coffee?" asked Dorothy when we reached the farmhouse. They hesitated. "Fancy you, a Chief Petty Officer's daughter, enticing them to leave their post," I whispered. A fragrant smell of grilled sausages wafting from the back door decided them. They came in and stayed an hour eating their share of the supper. I sincerely hoped that their absence was not discovered.

The latter part of November was cold and damp. On a day of finger-numbing rain from the north, Bill and I were ploughing the steeply sloping field under the Fort. The rain was not enough to stop us, but it made the chalk wet and slippery so that Lizzie's wheels spun and I was stuck on the hillside until, with sacks stuffed under the wheels, I could get her moving again.

My plough shares fell off with monotonous regularity and Lizzie joined in the fun by sooting up her plugs and passing out with coughs and splutters after every few turns of the field. Bill, seemingly oblivious of my problems, and having none of his own, ploughed up and down the field with irritating ease. About 4pm I lost the third plough share that afternoon. Searching back I found it half buried and prized it out of the sticky mud. When, as I hammered it on again I hit my thumb for the umpteenth time, the whole misery of the long, cold wet day caught up with me. I sat down in the soggy furrow and gave way to rare feminine tears.

Their effect on Bill was immediate. He stopped his tractor and came over. "There, there now," he crooned, in the manner of one soothing a small child. "You don't want to take on like that."

I continued to 'take on' for another minute or so while Bill looked helpless and searched through his pockets until he found a clean handkerchief. I had been cleaning Lizzie's plugs and wiping my filthy hands on mine.

"Here, blow your nose. Never could stand seeing a woman cry. Wot you want is a nice cup of tea." He fetched one from his thermos flask and a handful of rags from the supply he kept on his tractor. "Put these in your toolbox and you won't have to clean plugs with your handkerchief."

While I gratefully sipped the hot drink Bill fixed the plough share, started Lizzie and finished the furrow.

Then he took out the watch that he kept in a tobacco tin in his waistcoat pocket. "Only half an hour now to knocking off," he consoled me. "Just plough downhill 'til then."

"Why can't you never ask me to help you?" Bill muttered over his shoulder as we freewheeled our bikes down the hill on the way home. "Always so bloody independent!"

I didn't know. Although I always gratefully accepted help when it was offered it never occurred to me to ask. I had certainly come the long hard way round to realising that a man does not like a girl to be independent, even, or perhaps especially, if she is doing his job. In the future, whenever I got into difficulties I meekly sought Bill's assistance, and after that we got on splendidly.

In frosty weather we spent days muck-carting from the midden in the yard. It was easier to pull the laden trailers when the ground was hard. Also the frost broke down the manure making it easier to spread. I quite enjoyed this job on a clear, crisp morning and liked to see the brown mantle scattered over the white sparkling ground. Will could not understand why I got so much on my own person, plastering my prong handle, my gloves and the knees of my breeches.

"I 'low your breeks would stand up by themselves!" he declared.

"Don't you come in the house with those..." warned Mrs Coleby, "I'll bring down your others and you can change in the shed."

The worst aspect of the winter was the long dark evenings spent with the old couple in the comfortless kitchen. At the table, by the light of the oil lamp, I wrote letters home and sometimes to Dot Slightam, receiving lengthy replies written in a small, neat hand, which told me about Jack and the hounds, of their sons in the RAF and sometimes of the farm.

So the first months of winter passed. Because this year my job did not involve animals I was able to go home for four whole days at Christmas.

Tractor and plough out in the early morning, 1942.

CHAPTER 11

Cold Cures & Carthorses

The fact that I was always bareheaded, whatever the weather, worried the boss and his wife.

"You really should wear a hat," they admonished me. One raw wet morning the boss fetched an old trilby from a peg in the wash house.

Somehow I had lost my Land Army issue. "Here, put this on," he ordered. I wore it throughout the day and became attached to it. It had a friendly feel. From then on I wore it both in the field and the farm buildings.

"Once ee never wore no 'at. Now ee's never wi'out un!" old Will observed. The men, of course, never removed their own hats, except to wipe the sweat from their brows, revealing then a curious contrast between white forehead and brown face. After it had been soaked with rain a few times, blown off, and ploughed in, to be retrieved from the furrow on the next turn, my old trilby looked really rustic.

During my first two winters on the land, in spite of being often wet through and chilled to the marrow, I had remained consistently healthy. But not this winter, in spite of my protective headgear. One morning early in January I awoke with a sore throat and heavy head, and during the day developed the streaming nose, the bouts of violent sneezing and all the misery of a heavy cold.

"Nothing you can do for it" said Mrs Coleby briskly as I came down several mornings later with bleary eyes and congested tubes. "A cold has to take its course. Fresh air's the best thing." The air was certainly fresh on top of Portsdown where Bill and I were ploughing, but the bitter Northeaster did nothing to alleviate my discomfort. Twice during the morning Bill brought me a steaming cup of cocoa from his thermos and tea in the afternoon. Without his ministrations I would surely have perished.

"You want to wrap a sack round you," he said, fetching two from his tractor. He put one round my shoulders, piercing the corners with his penknife and tying them together with binder twine; another went round my waist covering my frozen knees. I felt warmer, although swathed in sacks with my battered hat pulled well down I would have deterred the most intrepid crow from the winter corn. At last my cold symptoms eased and gave way to a hacking cough, bringing sleepless nights and tiring days, with no more sign of abating than the bitter winds that persisted grey day after grey day. I was into the third week of it when, passing the farmhouse one morning on my way to the tractor shed, I was stopped in my tracks by a fit of coughing that would have made the Lady of the Camellias sound robust. At that moment Mrs Houghton opened the back door. "My goodness, haven't you lost that cough yet?" she called. I shook my head miserably. "Come in, I'll give you something to cure that." I went into the warm kitchen where the fragrance of bacon and egg still lingered and watched while she took a bottle from her preserve cupboard and removed the aged cork. The discoloured label read 'Blackcurrant Cordial'. She poured some into a saucepan on the stove and as it heated an aroma of many things beside blackcurrant wafted across to me; rum, brandy, orange and cloves.

"Good Lord, you're not giving her that stuff," exclaimed the boss, entering the kitchen.

"Why not?" replied his wife.

"Oh well," he shrugged as he pulled on his gum boots, "Kill or cure!"

Just then I did not particularly care which. Mrs Houghton poured some of the hot cordial into a glass and gave it to me, and the rest into a thermos flask. As I sipped it a delicious warm glow eased my aching throat and chest, reaching the spot that nothing else had touched, and spreading to the tips of my cold fingers and toes. Life suddenly took on a brighter aspect. Thanking my benefactress I put down the glass and took the thermos. When I reached the field I took another drink before hitching on the plough. This seemed a rather more difficult operation than usual and the ground appeared to be undulating a little as I climbed into the tractor seat, but I managed to keep the wheel straight in the furrow – so I thought – and every few turns of the field I took another sip of the magic elixir. It was when marking out a new ream that I really ran into trouble. Letting down the plough I had begun to steer for the marking stick at the other end of the field when suddenly there were three of them. I decided to aim for the middle one but then they began to float in a figure of eight; a sort of weaving dance. When I reached the end of the furrow three figures of Bill stood in a daunting row behind the three sticks. They took off their hats and scratched their heads and boomed at me.

"Wot's going on? Talk about a donkey's hind leg … more like the waves of the sea!"

"I think I'm a little drunk," I explained, "That cordial's pretty potent."

"I'm not surprised, I noticed you were swigging at it fairish. All right, go and finish my land – see if you can keep in the furrow. I'll try and straighten this out – and I won't report you for being drunk in charge of a tractor and plough!" he added with a grin.

"Reckon you can ride down the hill?" he asked at dinner time.

"Of course!" I replied, not feeling too sure. As I steered carefully down the steep incline I realised that I had not coughed once all the morning. After dinner I returned the thermos to Mrs Houghton. "How's the cough?" she asked.

"Gone, thank you" I replied. And it had. I was further cheered at the end of the month when a brand new tractor arrived for Bill and I had his old one, which was still a very great improvement on Lizzie. There was no more time wasted in starting her in the mornings. She was consigned to a corner of the barn where cobwebs made her a shroud and the sparrows whitened her with their droppings.

February lived up to its name of 'Fill Dyke' that year. It filled the road at the bottom of the hill to a depth of two feet. Like a delighted schoolboy, Bill got up speed on his bicycle and splashed through with his feet on the handlebars while I pedalled through at a more sober pace, cautious not to get the water over my gum boots.

When one morning the rain stopped and a pale wintry sun broke through the sombre cloud, Will said, "We're going to wind withs and bind bunts."

"Sounds fascinating" I replied.

"Makes a change," said Bill.

"How is it done?" I asked.

"You'll see."

I followed the two men to a corner of the field by the wood. Rows of faggots or bunts which Bill had been cutting out during the days of lighter rain, lay against the fence.

"Now, you takes a with, or withy," said Will, picking up a tough, flexible strip of willow, "put your foot on one end and twist ee round an round to split ee, then put ee on the ground and lay on your faggot. Then you twist back the splay end of the withy to make an eye. Thread t'other end through and pull ... and there ee is!"

He made it sound simple, but I was slow at the job and found it hard on the hands. My contribution to the neatly tied lot of bunts we later stacked onto the Bedford was small. We topped up the load with some green vegetables and the boss drove off to Portsmouth. It was the last trip for the old lorry. The boss, having disposed of the bunts, parked her in a street that led down to the harbour and went into a shop. When he came out she had disappeared.

"Looking for your lorry?" asked a passer by. "She's in there" and he jerked his thumb in the direction of the water. Her brakes had failed for the last time and she had slid gently and ignominiously into the drink, where only a few forlornly floating cabbages marked her watery grave.

I forget what replaced her, but I remember the sense of bereavement we all felt. She had been an integral part of the farm and it was never the same without her.

About this time two things happened to boost the morale of the Land Army. At the end of this fourth winter of the war we received our greatcoats. Very warm and smart they were too. Secondly, the long deferred decision had been made to admit WLA girls into NAAFI canteens. To mark these dual events, Dorothy and I cycled into Fareham, wearing our new coats, to visit the nearest NAAFI. At first, we sat alone and ignored in a corner, with our cups of tea and buttered toast and jam, feeling like country cousins, until we were joined by two other Land Girls who introduced themselves as Pamela and Maxine. They both worked on a large dairy farm the other side of Fareham and lived together in a houseboat on the river. We met them several times during that spring and one Sunday afternoon had tea with them on the houseboat. It was moored on the further side of the river which entailed rowing across in a small boat. Recalling how unwelcoming a country lane can be before dawn on a winter morning, I thought that negotiating a dark river at 5am called for a special nerve.

"You can never trust bulls" remarked Will one morning after Freddie Friesian had 'turned funny'. After years of apparent docility he had suddenly turned on Dorothy and chased her round the cowstalls. She had taken refuge in the dairy and remained there behind the firmly shut door until the boss came to her rescue. A week later Bill and I were walking back to the farm across the water meadows where we were repairing the bottom fence, when we saw Freddie coming toward us at a smart trot, head and tail at a threatening angle. I glanced at Bill. He appeared unconcerned, so we both walked steadily on while the distance rapidly narrowed between us and the menacing bull. When it was down to a few yards Bill threw up his arms and gave a shout. Freddie veered and trotted off in another direction.

"I was a bit nervous as to what was going to happen there!" I said, casually.

Bill grinned. "That makes two of us!" he replied.

When the bull cornered the boss in the yard and was driven off by Will with a pitchfork, he was finally deprived of his freedom.

"No, bulls is never to be trusted," said Will.

"Give me horses any day," said Maurice.

About that time I temporarily exchanged my tractor for Captain, and with the horse pulling the chain harrows I worked a small field above the hazel wood. The steady exercise of walking behind the harrows was a pleasant change from bouncing on the tractor; the smell of horse and leather a relief from the fumes of tractor fuel; the jingle of his harness and the regular soft thud of his feet on the loose ground sweeter on the ear than the roar and throb of an engine. I could hear a chaffinch trilling in the crab apple tree and the cry of the silver gulls as they rode the thermals. Maurice said that, as I was working with Captain, I might as well feed and groom him and pick out his hooves. He seemed quite happy to pass the general care of the old horse to me, but he would not have let anyone else look after the big black Shire mare, Bess; his pride and joy.

"The way he coddles that mare is ridiculous," the boss complained. "He puts all the rough work on old Captain. What she needs is a good hard day's work."

The fragile gentleness of April passed once more into the lush extravagance of May and we were again on the threshold of summer. Round again to the field weeding and hoeing and the sowing of the swedes and marigolds. I was now completely settled in my job and considered myself to be experienced in every phase of the year's work as it came round. I looked forward to the summer tasks. Then one morning Mrs Coleby told me in her usual brusque fashion that she no longer wanted anyone to look after and I must find other lodgings. My immediate reaction was one of relief; no more monotonous meals of warmed up meat and vegetables and unpalatable puddings of soaked cornflakes heated in the oven: no more uncomfortable evenings. It was quickly followed by dismay, for where among the few houses and cottages in the village would I find another billet? It was the same old problem. Enquiries brought offers of board; of breakfast from Bill's mother and other meals from the local policeman's young wife, but no lodging.

"I'd gladly have you here," she told me, "but we're not allowed to lodge people in the police house." In the end there seemed no alternative but to get another job. The boss had taken on an extra labourer in the spring, a genial, hardworking man in his forties. He would learn to drive my tractor. A new job was soon found for me on a small dairy farm near Winchester. A few days before I was due to leave, Bill arrived at work looking worried.

"What's up?" asked Maurice.

"My mother's ill" Bill told us. "Nothing serious, but she's got to stay in bed and there's hundreds of pinks to be picked for market tomorrow." Bill rented a large allotment in the village where he grew flowers for marketing. His mother picked, bunched and got them ready for the lorry that took them early into Portsmouth.

"Is there no-one to pick them for you?"

Bill shook his head. "I'll have to get up at dawn and pick them before I come to work."

"I'll help you," I said.

"See you on the allotment at 4am then," he grinned, only half believing in my offer which I had only half meant. When I woke the next morning it was still dark. I struck a match and looked at my alarm clock. A quarter-to-four. I did not feel like going back to sleep. Why should I not get up and help Bill with the pinks? Slipping out of bed I dressed quickly and quietly and silently lifted the latch of my bedroom door. On the stairs I carefully avoided those that creaked and just as noiselessly slid the bolts on the back door, and went out into the enveloping grey woolly blanket of the half darkness. I was first at the allotment and sat down on the grass to wait for Bill, acutely aware at first of the penetrating stillness. I could not see the pinks, but their scent, just before dawn, was as heady as the bouquet of a mature wine. Slowly a pink glow tinged the greyness and then "as soon as dawn with her rose coloured fingers lit the east" a blackbird quite close tried a few tentative notes. Another answered just as briefly, then another, like an orchestra tuning up. A moment later, from a robin came a robust whistle, while a song thrush added her melodious trill. Then, from every direction blackbirds joined in loud intrinsic harmony and the whole deafening chorus was under way. From the wood the cuckoo added his bell-like notes, while from some back garden a cockerel made his salutation to the dawn. I could now see the dark shadow of a belt of trees behind the allotment. The strengthening light revealed flowers and grass paths in strips of pink and green against the grey background, like a French Impressionist painting.

A church clock somewhere had chimed the half hour and it was almost light when I heard the gate click and Bill walked through pushing his bike.

"You're late!" I said from the shadow of the hedge.

He looked startled. "Didn't think you'd turn up."

"Well I did. Half-an-hour ago."

"Then what are you waiting for? Let's get started."

We picked the flowers in bunches of a dozen, tied them with bass and laid them end to end, the delicate pink blooms against hard blue stems, in a shallow basket. When this was full we transferred them to a crate fixed to Bill's bike. I thought the scent would stay in my nostrils for ever.

"How is your mother?" I asked.

"Oh, a lot better. Be up tomorrow, maybe."

We picked on in silence for an hour. The songbirds were silent now and the chorus was taken up by the woodpigeons. There were other sounds of life. A herdsman calling in the cows; a tractor starting up; a van being driven through the village. At 6 o'clock Bill straightened his back.

"I think that will about do," he said. We put the last bunches into the crate. Bill fastened the lid and we rode our separate ways to breakfast.

Mrs Coleby looked at me sharply as I entered the kitchen.

"Where do you think you've been?" she asked. When I told her she pursed her lips, then said curtly that I'd best get my breakfast, dumping my shredded wheat in front of me with such ferocity that it dumped out of the dish.

"I should not have gone out without telling you. I'm very sorry, but I woke early and couldn't sleep again. I didn't want to disturb you," I said.

"It was an impulse," I added, with partial truth. Mrs Coleby's snort of disdain told me what she thought of dawn impulses, but her husband, who evidently did not share her displeasure, looked at me with his gentle smile and said that daybreak was a lovely time to be out. I thought that by the end of the day Mrs Coleby's ire would have abated, but she continued to regard me in tight lipped silence until I left. I could not think why she should have been quite so angry, except that because of some old quarrel between the two families she disliked Bill.

I hated to part from anyone on bad terms and this added to my sadness at leaving the farm. When I had said my farewells all round the boss took me to the station where he had met me just fifteen months before.

"I'm sorry that you have to go," he said. "You handle any job on the farm as well as a man." It was praise indeed.

From the carriage window I watched the small white form of Midge as she followed him off the platform.

Land Army tractor drivers, 1941.

CHAPTER 12

Mary & Catherine

I stood looking up at King Alfred's statue through a veil of storm rain. He gazed back at me, grey as the sky behind him, benevolent but remote. As he could not tell me where the bus left for Stoke Charity I walked to the other side of the square where a small queue had gathered.

"Not to Stoke Charity dear, not at this time of day," replied a woman at the end of the queue. "Yes, this is the right bus, but it only goes as far as King's Worthy. You'll have to walk the rest".

"How far is it?" I asked.

"About four miles I should say. I hope it stops raining for you."

It had stopped raining by the time I got out of the bus at King's Worthy, but the atmosphere was close and humid, not the sort of day to carry a heavy case and holdall along interminable country lanes which seemed entirely deserted. Not a car passed in which I could beg a lift. For some while I walked along a straight road between fields of crops, many that were unfamiliar to me. Acres of yellow mustard, various grasses, many sown in evenly spaced rows. I afterward learned that the road divided two farms both of a thousand acres and both applying similar programmes which involved the growing of grass crops, Coltsfoot, S100, Timothy and others, for seed. Field after field they continued for a mile or so, broken only by a small copse or a belt of trees, without a building of any sort. So I was quite surprised when I suddenly came upon a long, low, thatched cottage built sideways onto the road and half concealed by trees. A sign read "Keeper's Cottage".

A tractor and trailer had just drawn up by the gate and two Land Girls got off. They came to meet me with friendly smiles as I walked over to ask if I was on the right road to Stoke Charity.

They were both fair haired and blue eyed, tanned and attractive. Mary, the tall slender one, was the gamekeeper's daughter. Catherine, her friend, an older girl, was of a shorter, broader build. Most noticeable was her expression of cheerful serenity.

"You're going to work for Mr Dance," said Mary. It was a statement, not a question. "Oh, everybody knows everything in the farming community. You look hot. Come in and have a cool drink."

It was a welcome suggestion. Inside I met Mrs Potts, Mary's mother, a comfortable, soft spoken Scotswoman and her father, formerly of the Scots Guards, who still retained his military moustache and bearing; an aged black labrador bitch lay at his feet. "She's m' Bess," he told me, noticing my interest in the dog. "She's totally blind but she follows me everywhere and will still retrieve. Last year when she still had a little sight, she won a field trial."

While I drank a tall glassful of squash Mary and Catherine told me about their work on the large, entirely mechanized farm.

I had seldom met two happier girls. Mary had been a court dressmaker but had taken to farm work with ease. Her fiancé was in the administrative side of agriculture. Catherine had worked in a bank and was to marry a former colleague, now a squadron leader in the RAF when he next had leave.

"The boss has just taken on a third Land Girl," said Mary. "She starts next week. It would be nice if you were coming to work here." I thought so too. It would be very nice to work on such a good farm with such congenial company. I was sorry to leave but I was bound for Stoke Charity and I must continue my walk. "Well, come and see us again," said Mr Potts. "You've about another two miles to go before you come to the village and Mr Dance's house is the first one on the left."

Stoke Charity was a tiny hamlet consisting of the farm, a few old cottages, a tiny church in the middle of a meadow, the Vicarage and some watercress beds. Beside the Vicarage, the farm was the only large house. Mrs Dance greeted me at the door with sympathetic concern.

"Oh dear, you didn't get the bus that comes all the way. You must be tired." She herself, although a strong-looking woman, had a pallor and air of utter fatigue. Later, I met her five lively and boisterous children, aged two to twelve, and understood why.

Mr Dance, who looked strong and vigorous enough to carry the world on his broad shoulders, did not come in from the field until supper.

"Oh, so you've come," was his brief greeting. "You'd better get to bed early. I want you up at the dairy at 5am prompt. I like people to be punctual in the morning." I set my alarm for 4.45 and I seemed to have scarcely closed my eyes before it went off.

The dairy was about a hundred yards up a lane from the farmhouse. When I got there I found it deserted and the gate locked. Obviously the rest of the dairy staff did not observe the boss's keenness for punctuality. I sat down on the grass verge, leaned against a wall and dozed until the cowmen arrived; first Ralph, the head man, who unlocked the gate and the dairy, then John, a quiet, handsome nineteen-year-old, and a Land Girl, Brenda, a buxom giggling blonde whose main aim in life I later found was to spend as much time as possible with the GIs from the local camp. She and John brought in the cows from the field. They were Ayrshires, about 25 in the herd, and my first introduction to the breed. I found them more attractive to look at than to work with. Their small, short teats were difficult to hold after the ample ones of the Shorthorn; they were none too careful with their long horns and they could kick so swiftly and suddenly than I seldom saw the movement of the leg that swept me off my stool. During milking times I seemed to spend a lot of time in the drain while the bruises on my shins increased daily. I wondered if Ralph, who seemed to take exception to me from the start, deliberately sat me under the worst kickers.

In contrast to the ill temper of his wives, William, the bull, was the kindest of creatures. A magnificent fellow, with noble head crowned with a bunch of curls, he was so gentle that four of the children could sit in a row on his back and ride him round the field.

I was always pleased when milking was over, the cows were turned out and I could return to the house for breakfast. By this time the boss had finished his breakfast and the general state of chaos and the piles of dirty crockery in the sink bore witness to the older children having been fed and got off to school. Mrs Dance was still seated at the table, her head supported wearily in her hands as if the operation had drained her of all vitality. She looked up half apologetically at not providing a breakfast for me.

"Can you open a tin of beans?" she asked languidly. I had never been over fond of that standby of the British diet, the baked bean, but I was, as usual, ravenously hungry. It was the same every morning, but because I was sorry for Mrs Dance, whose fatigue I could see was very genuine, as soon as I had demolished the last bean and several slices of bread and butter, I set about the pile of washing up which she showed no inclination to tackle, perhaps reserving her little remaining energy to cope with a demanding toddler when he awoke.

A little outhouse by the back door contained a tall, old fashioned pump and here I repaired after breakfast to pump water to the upstairs tank in the house and the water tough in the field adjoining the garden. The upward stroke of the long handle took the full extent of my reach, the downward came to my feet. It took about half-an-hour's pumping to fill the house tank and often more to fill the trough.

"It must be full to the brim when you stop," the boss insisted, "no matter how many cows come to drink."

It was the cows coming to drink that prolonged the job, which in time took on the dimension of an army fatigue or the tread-wheel in the 19th century house of correction. When the trough was almost full one would amble over and drink deeply, faster than I could pump, then another, while the water level sank rapidly. When at last the procession ended and I could see water shining on the brim I rushed away before another four-legged water tank should come up for a refill.

Besides Ayrshires the boss also bred Clydesdale/Shire cross horses, and had at that time a stallion named Bob, two brood mares and a filly. They were handsome animals, rich bay in colour and longer, cleaner legged than the pure Shire. Bob was a splendid fellow, over eighteen hands high with a small white star on his wide forehead.

"Have you had any experience with horses?" the boss asked me one morning at breakfast when I had been at the farm a week. Rather recklessly as it turned out, I told him that I could ride and about the milk round and the work I had done with Captain.

"Fine," he said. "When you've finished at the pump you can take Bob and get a load of hay. He's in the stable. Groom him first, then put him in the cart – it's in the yard – and in the field opposite Ralph's cottage you'll see a last year's hay rick that's been cut out. Get a load and put it in the shed by the calves. You'll find the hay cutting knife stuck in the rick."

With such explicit directions where could I go wrong?

Bob looked big in the field; in the stable he looked enormous. I gazed in awe at his great strength and height.

"Oh yes," I had said with confidence, "I know how to put on the harness." What I did not know was how I would reach to put the collar over Bob's head. A quick search of the yard produced an old upturned bucket, probably used by someone similarly lacking in stature. By teetering on this I just managed to put on the collar and fasten the hames. He was a 'gentle giant' and submitted quietly to being groomed, harnessed, and hitched into the cart, but once I was up behind him and picked up the reins he took off like a rocket from a launch pad. Our rapid exit from the yard was a hit or miss affair that left the gate post shuddering. We bowled along at a splendid pace, Bob lifting his great feet high in a fast trot, scarcely slackening speed on the sharp bend by the farmhouse. Luckily we met no other vehicles, only an old man on a bicycle who leapt into the hedge with remarkable agility. Bob obviously knew the routine and swung into the gateway by Ralph's cottage, the nearside wheel of the cart again bouncing off the post. He stopped by the rick and backed up without a word of command from me. Climbing the ladder I found the hay knife and had cut out several squares of crisp hay and pitched them down into the cart when I heard the sound of a horse's hooves on the road. Bob heard them too, and pricked up his ears. A moment later a man rode by on a good-looking mare. She put Bob's mind clean off his work. Regardless of the cart behind him he cantered after her, following as closely as he could from the other side of the hedge until he was checked at the corner of the field. There he stayed leaning into the restraining hawthorn while his impassioned whinnying reverberated down the lane. I got down and led him back to the rick, but before I reached the top of the ladder again he was back at the corner. When this had happened twice more I decided that the mountain must come to Mahomet. Pitching the remainder of the cut hay onto the ground I carried it, as much as I could get on a pitchfork at a time, to the cart. It vas a slow, laborious process. When I had completed my load Bob was very willing to take the road home, for that was the direction in which the mare had disappeared. He settled down by the time I reached the yard and stood quietly while I unloaded the hay. Soon now I would have him safely tied up in the stables. But when I opened the door he charged through with such force that I let go of the halter rope and jumped aside to save my toes. The reason for this unseemly haste was soon apparent. Someone, with lamentable lack of foresight, had tied the two mares, Bertha and Belle, in the end stalls. In the ensuing cacophony of squealing and whinnying, stamping and lashing of hooves, I lost my nerve, slammed the stable door and fled. I met a scowling Ralph in the gateway. Brushing me aside he rushed to the stable. I left him to it.

Late as I was, my dinner had not spoiled with keeping, for it was that stand-by of our diet – cold, fat bacon. The previous year, the children had reared a pig called Jimmy. They loved him dearly and fed him too well, with the result that when he was killed he weighed eighteen score and was solid fat. Although the children refused to eat the flesh of their former pet over whose demise they had wept copiously, Mr & Mrs Dance and I ate it for dinner most days of the week. Milk being plentiful this was followed by rice or macaroni pudding or a huge treacle tart with clotted cream that Mrs Dance made in large quantities from the rich produce of the Ayrshires. On such a diet I could have acquired the proportions of the deceased Jimmy himself had I not worked such long and energetic hours. My morning exercise at the pump alone prevented me from putting on weight and now that it was haymaking time once more, I pitched hay all the hours I was not working in the dairy, until 9 o'clock to 10 o'clock at night, six days a week and up to tea time on Sundays. The WLA wage was now 45/- for a 51 hour week. As I was working at least 95, my weekly wage with overtime exceeded £5. Wealth indeed!

We carried the hay with wagons and horses and one Massey Harris 101 tractor and trailer. I had not worked with Bob since the rick episode. The boss had not been at all pleased about him being let in with the mares and it took a little time to reinforce the gateposts. I did some harrowing with Belle, who at a mere 16 hands high and of a quiet disposition was easy to manage. Then one afternoon the boss told me to take Bob down to the lower meadow where I would find a hay rake.

"If you can rake that bit up before tea we can get it picked up this evening," he said.

After an energetic caper across two fields trying to keep up with Bob's jog trot as he would not accommodate his pace to mine, we arrived at the meadow where I tied him to a tree while I looked for the hay rake. I found it in the hedge where it had probably spent the winter. It was in a sorry state; the wheels wobbled; the little iron seat was loose and the long lever which raised the tines to release the hay was stiff and creaking, while the whole thing when moved, squeaked and chirruped like a cage full of budgerigars. It would not be a comfortable ride. Furthermore I could see from the start that I was in for mare trouble again, for Bertha and Belle were turned out in the adjoining meadow.

Bob had already observed them and as I hitched him into the shafts and climbed onto my high, precarious seat, he edged towards the fence, while they came over very sociably to greet him. He was reluctant to leave them and his progress down the field was the ultimate in slow motion, but at the end he turned like a show jumper before the last fence and cantered full pelt back to the mares, while I pulled on the reins with one hand and attempted to operate the difficult lever with the other, at the same time keeping an uncertain balance on the rickety seat. This performance was reiterated throughout the long, hot afternoon; the funeral progress down the field, the hazardous turn and the charge up the field at a pace Ben Hur would not have attempted in a decrepit hay rake. I gave up trying to lift the lever at regular intervals, with the result that instead of long, straight lines of hay, evenly spaced to allow the wagons to pass between, there were untidy heaps of assorted sizes dotted at random all over the field. The boss was scathing in his comments when he saw the result of my afternoon's work.

"I don't know why you can't manage the horse," he said, "I broke him as a colt and I've never had any trouble with him."

I thought the fact that he was a very large, strong man, with a lifetime's experience with heavy horses might have something to do with it.

When haymaking was over work became easier. Half days were restored and evenings were free. I even had several Sunday afternoons off when I accompanied Mr & Mrs Dance and the children to his father's farm near Andover. Along the road was a riding establishment with some good horses, and while the boss spent the afternoon with his family I explored some rides across the Wiltshire Downs, returning to the farm for tea.

One of the several advantages of living in the farmhouse as opposed to a billet was the very kind hospitality one often received from the farmer's family and friends. I renewed my acquaintance with Mary and Catherine and Mr & Mrs Potts and spent several evenings at the Keeper's Cottage. Catherine was now married to her Squadron Leader and had just returned from honeymoon. The third girl had settled in on the farm. The pheasant's fluffy, speckled chicks that Mr Potts had shown me clustered in incubators on that first day I stopped at the cottage, were now young birds running in wire cages. This tall ex-guardsman personified the best type of gamekeeper, with a deep understanding of his job and country lore, of guns and the sympathetic training and care of dogs. I have since met many gamekeepers, but few of his calibre.

While at Stoke Charity I had my second encounter with sheep. At his other farm at Inkpen on the Berkshire Downs, Mr Dance kept a flock of Southdowns and one day after haymaking the family and I went over for the shearing. Mrs Dance rose early and prepared bottles of lemonade and biscuit tins full of fat bacon sandwiches, then she and I and the five children piled into the big, old Buick. Mr Dance threw a couple of sheepdogs in on top, got in himself, and we set off through the lovely countryside of the Hampshire-Berkshire border. After about an hour's driving we reached the ridge of the Downs that overlooks Newbury, where the old gibbet stood silhouetted against the skyline, a grim reminder of the days when highwaymen were hung in chains. The farm lay in the valley. Here we found half the flock penned in readiness at one end of the big barn. At the other end was collected the shearing tackle; three pairs of mechanical shears which were operated by a hand turned wheel, and a platform where the fleeces were rolled and stacked. I worked first of all with the resident Land Girl, Alison, who was small and wiry but incredibly strong and capable. Together we caught the sheep and lifted them over the hurdle for the shearers. This was a simple enough job until the sheep got fewer and had more room for evasion. The last few proved as elusive as goldfish in a bowl. While we broke for lunch, sitting on straw bales to eat our sandwiches, the remainder of the flock were got in. Throughout the afternoon Alison rolled and weighed the fleeces and I turned the wheel for the shearers, getting liberally splattered with oil from its cogs in the process. Then it was my turn at the fleeces, which weighed on average five to six pounds each. The lanolin from the wool as I folded and tied them did wonders for my work-roughened hands. At the end of the day, as a special treat, I was allowed to shear two wethers.

"Get ee settin' comfortable, then ee won't be no trouble," the old shepherd instructed me, as I tentatively handled the first one. Having grown accustomed to the vibration of the shears in my hand, I soon got the hang of the job, keeping the shears close to the skin I watched the fleece falling softly away, revealing pink skin beneath the close cropped wool.

"Thet ain't bad," said Shep when I'd finished. "Thet ain't bad at all." When the last sheep was sheared and turned out we went into the farmhouse to wash, then sat down at the long dining room table to a sumptuous tea that the manager's wife had provided.

We drove home in the mellow summer evening, five year old Mary asleep on my lap, the head and fore paws of a sleeping collie on my shoulder, the rest of its body reclining in the back window; another dog curled up on my feet. When we got home Ralph was waiting to tell the boss that the old mare had dropped her foal and, tired as we were, the older children and I went to see it. Dark coloured like its dam and wobbly legged, it was suckling; a sight that made a pleasing end to a happy day.

Although days like this and my Sunday rides were currants in the cake, there was the other side. In the cowpens, Ralph still made my work difficult. He had an unpleasant habit when I was untying a cow, of loosing the one next to it so it swung round, scoring my back with its sharp horns. There were the hours at the pump and hair-raising episodes with Bob. At the farm where Mary and Catherine worked the atmosphere was happy and relaxed, the work so well organised that I wished very much that I could work there instead. There had seemed very little chance of this, when, quite suddenly, owing to illness in her family the third Land Girl left. A sympathetic WLA representative organised a transfer and found a billet for me with a pleasant woman whose husband was with the Forces in Sicily. I started my new job on the fourth day of August.

Thatching a rick.

CHAPTER 13

Accident Prone

It was good to sleep for an extra hour in the morning. At six o'clock the sun was streaming in through the tiny window under an eyebrow of thatch. The house martins were chattering in the eaves.

I got out of bed and looked out across the cottage garden and the narrow lane to the line of graceful alders that fringed the water meadows. There was a brook full of meadowsweet and purple loosestrife, where the yellow iris had bloomed earlier in the year. As I dressed, the fragrant smell of bacon frying wafted up to me. At last, that cooked breakfast! I quickly tidied the room before I left it. It was small but daintily and adequately furnished and scrupulously clean. The whole cottage smelt sweetly of soap and polish and lavender. Mrs Simmons, my new landlady, filled in her lonely days by taking meticulous care of the little home she had not long shared with her husband before he was called up. She was not young, nor very strong.

"I cannot go out and do war work," she told me, as I tucked into bacon and eggs, the latter from the few fowls she tended in the garden. "But I have always looked after a Land Girl. Most of them worked on the water cress beds. They none of them stayed very long."

Working with watercress was, no doubt, tedious, wet and sometimes cold, but after I had been with Mrs Simmons a few days I could not think that anyone would wish to leave her care once they had sampled her cooking, for she had a clever and imaginative way of producing varied and satisfying meals from our rations.

The farm where I now worked differed vastly from the one I had just left. Whereas animals abounded there – horses, cattle, sheepdogs, the children's donkey and other pets – on this farm there was not even a cat. Mr McMorland, known affectionately among his employees as Mac, had an impressive muster of the most up-to-date machinery. Here I saw the first machine to dig, sort and bag potatoes in its progress round the field, and I had my first introduction to the combine harvester. A full time mechanic was employed to ensure that it was all meticulously maintained so that there was the minimum of breakdowns to disrupt the work and a machine was always ready for use when it was needed. Mary drove a Massey 101 tractor and Catherine and Will, an elderly man who had worked for many years on the farm, a big Massey 45. Mine was a brand new John Deere Rowcrop, with six forward gears: three in high ratio, three in low. There was a certain amount of trial and error in sorting out this more complicated gearbox, but eventually I got it right. The basic purpose of the Rowcrop tractor was the field hoeing of the grass crops. Many hours were spent on this task in early summer, but as hoeing was finished for this year I never had the opportunity to try it out on this work.

We four drivers each kept a log book of our tractor working hours, of services and oil changes that were done, with unfailing regularity. I had never before met with quite such careful routine and organisation, and with this smooth running efficiency was a pleasant harmony and camaraderie among the staff. Mary was perhaps the most capable and independent of us girls. The fingers that before the war had executed the finest needlework now expertly handled the changing of the big wheels on her tractor, a job few men attempted without help, changing the oil or lifting heavy drawbars to hitch implements onto her machine.

Soon after my arrival the combine harvester moved into a thirty acre field of wheat. Mary with her tractor pulled the machine, which resembled a tall ship sailing smoothly through a sea of golden corn. I stood on top, like a monkey on a barrel organ, to ensure that the wheat flowed evenly into the drum. A second combine, one of the first to be self motivated and with the fans in front so that it could enter the corn at any angle, was driven by Will. Catherine, with her tractor and a large trailer took the corn from the drums when full and drove it to the drier in the big barn. Sitting waiting in the hot sun she invariably fell sound asleep over the steering wheel and Mary had to walk over to wake her when it was time to empty the drums.

The mustard, too, was ready to harvest and Mary and I were taken off the wheat to spend a day combining the crop. It was difficult stuff to combine. With its rough, wiry stalks and pods it stuck to the platform and clogged the rollers, and we spent as much time unclogging and pulling out the tangled mass as we did in progress round the field. Even this did not seem to try Mary's patience, for she had the same calm, happy temperament as Catharine, coupled with a sense of fun that made both girls splendid companions to work with.

Employed on the farm during the harvest was a family of gypsies. Tom, a black-haired, swarthy, mountain of a man, who wore a massive leather belt like a horse's girth, decorated with brass emblems, and his two daughters, Tilly and Lena. Tilly was surprisingly small and dainty with dark hair worn in long ringlets, while her sister was a big built, brassy blonde, which, I decided, could not be her natural hair colour. They all worked in the drier and toward the end of harvest Will and I joined them and spent our days wheeling and tipping the heavy sacks of wheat to load the continuously waiting lorries. There was a unique atmosphere in the drier. Coming into it from the sunlight of the field it was dim except for the fierce glow of the roaring furnace. Overhead was a complication of belts and pulleys, while a deep pit contained a shifting abyss of brown wheat. There was a smell of coke fumes and warm new corn. In the doorway, myriad particles of dust danced and whirled in a shaft of sunlight. As the sacks of dried wheat were loaded onto lorries at one side of the barn, Catherine brought in more trailer loads from the field at the other, and still the combines made their steady progress round the fields. It was while working in the drier that the happy time I had spent on the farm came to a sudden and unexpected end.

In my youth I was accident prone. I was either falling heavily onto something hard, or standing in the way of something hard and heavy that was falling. One afternoon in mid-September all work ground to a halt when the drier seized up. Catherine waited with a trailer load of wheat which she was unable to unload and the combines with full tanks ceased their circuit of the fields. While the mechanic worked Catherine and I stood talking by the drier pit. Eventually the engine started and belts slowly began to rotate again. Suddenly I was stunned by a blow to the base of my neck. I felt myself reeling across the floor in a receding haze of shock and bewilderment ... then blackness. When I came round I was looking into Catherine's anxious face. There was a searing pain in my back, and more alarming, for what seemed an interminable time, I was unable to breathe. I was also very hot. Someone who had learned that a person in shock should be kept warm had covered me with heavy West of England sacks. Catherine removed all but one and wiped my forehead with a cool, fragrant handkerchief. From time to time other faces loomed up through the haze, Mac's looking desperately worried; Will's showing concern, and then a doctor's. From Mac's murmured explanation to him I learned that a pulley wheel had fallen from the top of the drier onto my back. "It dropped twenty feet..." I heard him say. (Will put it on the scale afterwards. It weighed seventy-five pounds.) Then ambulance men, quiet and efficient, lifting me skilfully onto a stretcher. Catherine came with me in the ambulance to Winchester Hospital and I was grateful for the comfort of her reassuring presence. She waited with me in casualty, where there were more seemingly unattached faces, of nurses and a young houseman, until I was taken to a ward. It took several X-rays to satisfy the orthopaedic specialist about my injuries. Meanwhile I was treated as a fractured spine. Days passed while I waited to know whether I would spend the next nine months in plaster like the woman two beds away.

"You'll have to be patient," said Sister, "X-ray is very busy. There are more important cases."

I knew these to be wounded and injured servicemen who filled several wards in the hospital. As it turned out I was lucky. Because of the rapid spinning of the wheel as it fell, the blow had been but a glancing one, resulting in nothing more serious than a cracked vertebra, two broken ribs and concussion.

"We always knew you were a fraud," said Staff Nurse, smiling.

After the third week I was allowed to sit up and was moved onto a glass covered balcony that overlooked the town and the tree capped dome of St Catherine's Hill. My companions were WAAFs and ATS of my own age recovering from orthopaedic operations. As I was the only one still not mobile they gathered round my bed and we talked and played Lexicon by the hour. I missed them all very much when I was discharged and went home to begin a long convalescence.

By November I was feeling pretty fit and accepted an invitation from Dot Slightam to spend a week or two at the kennels. It was strange to be back in my old room again; to be among familiar sights and sounds. Everything was the same and yet not the same, as a place always feels after a timely absence. As before, Jack talked over supper of horses and hounds and told hunting stories, but something, or someone, was missing. But the rain was just as I remembered it, falling heavily and persistently with the last of the brown leaves, dripping from bare branches and lying in pools on the rides. Despite the inclement weather I got in some riding at a stables in Lyndhurst and walks with Dot and with Jack and a much-reduced pack of hounds. There was no hunting that winter.

The last morning I stayed indoors, watching a deluge that almost obliterated the view from the living room window. That was the way it had rained on so many days during the harvest of 1941; that summer when there had been a full pack of hounds in the kennels, Percy had grazed in the paddock and Richard had cycled across the fields most evenings to supper. I wondered where he was now and would have given much to know. I had little doubt that he would have got his pilot's wings and I wondered in what aircraft and on what operations he was flying.

"For goodness sake Jose, stop staring out of that window," said Dot, as if divining my thoughts, "Jack is just going out with the hounds. Put on a mac and go with him."

At the end of the month I returned to Winchester, staying a few miles out from the town in the McMorland's home on the River Itchen. I was due for a final check up with the orthopaedic consultant. He pronounced me sound in wind and limb, but made one proviso. I was to do no more farm work. My face must have registered my utter dismay.

"Well, perhaps a very light job," he conceded. There were no light jobs in farming, I told him. I was either fit for normal work or not.

"Then you're not," he said emphatically. "I will write to your employer and tell him."

The letter arrived a few days later, Mac read it gravely. "I'm afraid, in the face of this I am unable to take you back," he said.

"But I have no intention of leaving the Land Army" I replied vehemently. "If I don't work for you I shall apply for another job".

But Mac was adamant. "That must be your decision, but I cannot keep you on."

I had been eagerly anticipating a return to work, to tractor driving again and to the renewed company of Mary and Catherine. Now I was faced with yet another fresh start.

Although Mac had been informed of the specialist's decision, the WLA County Headquarters had not and they had no compunction about finding me a new job straight away. It was assisting the stockman with the care and feeding of 1,500 head of dry stock on a 5,000 acre farm near Winchester. My billet was in a farmhouse with the arable foreman and his wife, and I was to start right away.

I was back in the farming business.

CHAPTER 14

Meeting Duggan

The weather was cold and grey that first week in December and as I broke the ice on the cattle trough at 7am to fill the radiator of my tractor, I reflected that I was back on the land indeed. I was happy to be at work again, nonetheless, after nearly three months sick leave.

My first job was to load up a trailer with bales of straw from the Dutch barn and a sack of cow nuts from the granary and feed thirty heifers in the adjoining field while Ernest, the stockman, did a round of all the dry stock on the farm on his motorbike. I received these instructions as I left the farmhouse, from the dairy foreman, a lean, wiry, ginger haired Scotsman known as Jock, who looked at me with amusement in his twinkling blue eyes.

"And be shure they're all there," he added.

After wrestling with a tightly fastened barb wire gate, I drove into the field. While I secured the gate, again with difficulty, the heifers trotted over eagerly to meet their breakfast. Leaving the tractor to steer itself I climbed onto the trailer and released a trail of nuts and then of straw, leaping back onto the tractor now and then when she headed for the fence or a rabbit warren. I left counting the cattle until they were nicely spread out along the line of straw and fairly stationary. I made it thirty at the third count and checked once more. They gazed up at me, straw hanging from their mouths like long yellow moustaches.

"By the time you get back to the barn, Ernest will be there to load up with you for your main feed round," Jock had said. But it was five minutes or more before a tall, thin faced man arrived, dressed in a voluminous raincoat tied round the waist with binder twine, and huge gumboots. I had already loaded up two layers of bales.

"Ah, good, getting on with it I see," he remarked. This I found out later was my first mistake. Together we put up seventy bales. These, when dry, weighed about 95 pounds each and were heavier when wet. I managed by building the load in steps and rolling them up so that I had to lift only the last ones with the bale crook. Even so, it was hardly what my orthopaedic specialist would have called 'light work' and I am perhaps fortunate that never have I suffered from so completely disregarding his advice!

The farm, an amalgamation of several farms, was vast. Besides two thousand acres of arable land there were five dairies and five milking bails with more cattle, Friesian and Ayrshire, than I had ever seen. Although we covered only a portion of it on our round we travelled about fifteen miles and the feeding took four hours, even if we had no hindrances such as stopping to calve a cow or help the farm lorry driver to load up a sick animal or a cow and calf, which frequently happened. Ernest always drove the tractor while I perched on the corner of the trailer, jumping down as we approached a field to struggle with the wire gate (I had never before fully appreciated nice wooden gates with hinges) cut open the wire tied bales and throw off the straw. Once a week on Ernest's day off, Tom, one of the arable staff, came on the round in his place. Then I drove and he rode the trailer and opened the gates. I liked Ernest's days off and I liked Tom, an older man, who had for many years worked as a shepherd and had that gentle wisdom of most of his kind.

We stopped en route at barns and straw stacks in the fields to replenish our load. One day, while loading up at a Dutch barn I picked up a bale and came face to face with a barn owl. We stared at each other for a moment, he with wide unblinking eyes. I apologised for disturbing him, replaced the bale and took another.

Another time when with Tom I uncovered a nest of dormice, tiny reddish brown creatures huddled together with their long bushy tails curled around them.

"We calls 'em the seven sleepers," Tom told me, "because they sleeps seven months of the year. Cover 'em up. We won't disturb 'em. Pretty little things." I thought that Ernest would not have shown concern for dormice. His only interest in wildlife was its potential for the pot. He was a keen pigeon shooter, either for a pie or to sell in Winchester, where they fetched 2/6d each at the butchers. A rabbit crouching under uneaten straw in the fields did not escape Ernest's keen eye. Putting the tractor into top gear he would roar down upon it and leaning over the mudguard, stun the petrified animal with his prong. Then, on his instruction, I jumped off the trailer and picked it up by its back legs and gave it to him to be dispatched. He and his wife enjoyed many a rabbit stew acquired in this way.

My afternoons were spent cutting kale for the dairy herds. That first day, after the frost, came heavy rain. It started as we came back from the round and by mid afternoon had become a deluge. It poured off the brim of my hat as I bent over the bill hook and seeped under the collar of my raincoat. It ran off the broad leaves of the kale into my gumboots. I was wetter than a coastguard on a storm-swept cliff. Jock drove his van across the field, the wheels spinning in the mud, and got out to see how I was getting on.

"Aye, ets a bugger," he commented cheerfully. "You don't seem t' mind getting wet, though," he added as I returned his smile, amused by his greeting. I found on further acquaintance that Jock's speech was usually well littered with expletives, while on really stressful occasions his oaths could be rich, varied and blasphemous. But delivered in his Scots brogue and with a twinkle in his eye they were never offensive.

Jock had a lovely wife, tall and slender with delicate features and beautiful violet eyes. Her name was Vi and they had two schoolboy sons, the elder tall and good looking like her and the other a ginger haired mischievous rascal like his father.

Algie and his wife, with whom I was billeted, were a very different couple. He was very dark and quiet while she was auburn haired, energetic and vivacious. They were both extremely kind and after long, wet or cold days on the farm I enjoyed their fireside as I sat with my interminable sock mending, while Mrs Collins knitted, their schoolgirl daughter wrestled with her homework, and Algie and Geoffrey, the young assistant who also lived in the farmhouse, discussed the business of the arable side of the farm. I was perhaps happier than I had been anywhere since the days at the Kennels.

The highlight of the week was the farm social. The boss had built, for this purpose, a large hall next to the buildings at the Home Farm. Here the farm staff of forty strong, with their wives, met every Friday night during the winter months to dance, play darts or billiards, or just talk at the bar where beer and soft drinks were provided. The cattle lorry, which afforded transport to the hall was thoroughly scrubbed out by Bill, the driver, and lined with bales of straw for the women to sit on while the men balanced the best they could in the centre. Tarpaulins hung against the slatted sides excludes most of the wind and rain. In spite of these cosy arrangements I was glad when Geoff offered me a lift in his van as an alternative to the lorry.

Gradually that winter, a few GIs from the local camps filtered in to join the social gathering. Americans, both black and white, were much in evidence in the village and the steady traffic of their jeeps and trucks and lorries was often a hazard to be met with when driving a tractor and loaded trailer along a narrow lane, but only once was I forced off the road and into the ditch. With their smart uniforms, their persuasive manners and seemingly endless supply of nylons, cigarettes and candy, they were extremely popular with both the local girls and the children.

During the summer there were one or two weddings at the village church. I could not help wondering what the future held for these girls who could have known so little of their husband's backgrounds. A few GIs who came from farms were interested in our farming methods. Two who turned up at the Dutch barn on a number of mornings seemed singularly interested in watching me load the trailer.

"You wouldn't get girls back home to work like that," they declared. I began to think that I was working a little too hard, for Ernest seldom appeared in the mornings until I had put up the last bale, then always full of excuses about calving cows, missing heifers or cattle to load. It was not until I called at his house with a message one morning and saw him drinking tea and reading the paper with his feet on the mantelpiece that I realised the real reason for his tardiness. After his considerable embarrassment on this occasion he arrived most mornings in time to help me load.

No sooner had I got into the swing of my new job than it was Christmas. Ernest had Christmas Day off. Geoff went home for the whole holiday and Algie and family spent the day with friends at Fleet, leaving at 8am and not returning until midnight.

Tom came with me on the feed round. To be working when most people have the day off is a lonely experience. Even the dairy staff had finished early and gone home. Returning to the farmhouse I cooked a solitary lunch of bacon and eggs, glad of the company of Rusty, the Collins's little mongrel dog which I was looking after for the day. In the afternoon I walked with him through a deserted countryside. Everyone in the village, it seemed, was indoors listening to the radio, or sleeping after their Christmas dinner. All day I had been looking forward to the evening which Catherine had invited me to spend with her family. I made myself some tea, fed Rusty, changed and cycled into Winchester. Catherine lived in one of the tall semi-detached houses that lined a steep hill leading down to the town. As I climbed the steep steps to the front door I thought that the house seemed very quiet. There was little evidence of the party of young relatives, one or two on leave from the forces, that I had expected. There was no reply to my knock. I tried again, louder. The house was silent. I looked down the street. It was in total darkness, but behind heavy blackout curtains there were warm, light rooms where folk were celebrating Christmas night. I knocked once more. It was a big house, perhaps everyone was out of earshot. It was unlike Catherine to have forgotten having asked me. Perhaps she had to fall in with other family plans and had not been able to let me know. No-one answered. I had no alternative but to go back to the cold, empty farmhouse, find something to read and go to bed. As I turned away a little old man appeared at the wall which separated the garden from the one next door. Wearing a velvet smoking jacket and smoking cap with a long tassel, with pince-nez on his thin nose, he might have stepped straight out of a Dickens novel.

"I'm afraid there is no-one in," he said in a quavering voice. I told him who I was and why I was there.

"Oh dear, dear. That's a pity," he exclaimed. "You know, my sister and I are all alone. We would like it very much if you would spend the evening with us." It would have been churlish to refuse so gracious an invitation and, even if it was not quite the evening I had anticipated, it must be better than returning straight home. Indoors the old gentleman took my coat and ushered me into a dimly lit room furnished in Victorian style with heavy furniture, dark crimson wallpaper, antimacassars on the chairs and a fringed drape on the mantelpiece. His sister looked even older and more frail than he and wore a long black taffeta dress with a high neck such as my grandmother would have worn. She received me in shy, gentle manner.

"Perhaps we can find a drop of sherry," said her brother, shuffling to the sideboard and producing three dusty glasses and a bottle of thick dark sherry which could have seen many a Christmas. As we sipped the treacly liquid and made polite conversation I felt as if I had taken a trip backward on a time machine, and wondered how we were going to pass the long evening.

"What about a game of cards?" the old gentleman suggested, producing a well worn pack. We played the old games of Rummy and Snap and all got quite excited over Beat-Your-Neighbour-Out-of-Town. When several clocks had struck the hour of nine I got up to go.

"Oh, not yet" said the old man. "My sister will get a little something to eat, won't you, my dear?" The old lady repaired to the kitchen, returning with a plate of sandwiches and three cups of Camp Coffee. An hour later I thanked them very much for their hospitality and said that I really must go.

"Thank you" replied the old man. "You have made our Christmas". He insisted on coming out into the cold night and seeing me onto my bicycle. As I pedalled home I realized that I did not even know their name and felt that the whole evening had an atmosphere of unreality. When I next saw Catherine she did not mention Christmas night. I could only think that in the excitement of having her husband and her brother home on leave she had completely forgotten her invitation.

Boxing Day was my day off. I got up early to catch the milk lorry which on its journey to the coast went through New Milton and the driver had promised me a lift. Getting back would involve a slow difficult train journey and perhaps a walk from Winchester, but at least I would have a belated Christmas dinner with my mother.

The days varied little during the early months of the New Year. The weather was alternatively wet or cold but there was no snow. As I loaded bales from the stacks in the fields the front of my corduroys became wet from frost or rain, and as I sat on the trailer in the icy wind they often froze to my legs. It was the only time I have ever had chilblains on my knees. Cutting frozen kale in the afternoons was a finger nipping job. As I rubbed some life into my numbed extremities I dreamed of spring.

I was fully experienced now in calving cows and had helped with various incorrect presentations, hind legs first, head or a foreleg back. But a job that still baffled me was picking out the 'springers' – heifers 'springing' or just about to calve. They had to be taken out of the bunch and loaded onto the lorry to be taken to whichever dairy they belonged. The first way of telling was by the development of the udder.

"Now, *she's* a springer," I would say, pointing out one to Bill, the lorry driver.

"Rubbish!" he would reply, "She's got another six weeks to go!"

In the end I gave up and left it to the experts.

Because there was little to talk about during the dull winter days but the weather and the war news, any new arrival in the village or on the farm was of great interest and they were discussed by the men and their wives, at the meal table and by the fireside, until every detail of their appearance and all that could be found out about their background and former occupation had been gone over with the maximum thoroughness. The latest victim of this scrutiny was Jock's new assistant who arrived in March.

"He's a handsome chap," Algie remarked one dinnertime, with a meaningful glance at me. "Tall too."

"Another Scot, so they say," replied his wife. "Can't be. His name's Rees."

"Oh, a Welshman then."

"His home's in Wales but he doesn't sound Welsh."

"What's his Christian name?" asked Mrs Collins.

"I don't know. He likes to be called Duggan but that's part of his surname. It's a sort of double barrelled name."

"Jock says he's a 'bi' o' a torff," Geoff volunteered a first remark with a fair imitation of Jock's accent.

"He certainly dresses well," said Algie, "and he doesn't wear gum boots but sort of fitted rubber riding boots."

The boots, more than anything else about this young man seemed to impress the entire farm staff.

One dinnertime, Algie came in bursting with a story of how Duggan, after an altercation with the tough, surly, fifteen-stone Irishman at Bail 5 had "socked him on the jaw and laid him out." The fact that anyone had confronted Paddy, let alone knocked him down was a nine days' wonder. It provided a tasty morsel of conversation on the farm for several days while the men eyed Duggan with a new respect and some apprehension. He had, it transpired, some useful experience with the gloves.

Because in due course it was discovered that Duggan was unmarried and unattached and I was the only girl on the farm, a great deal of matchmaking went on. The more I remained aloof from any discussion of this sort the more determined Jock and Algie became that I should show some interest in the new arrival. The fact that his thick, dark, curly hair was greying at the temples gave rise to much speculation regarding his age.

"Must be over thirty," said Algie. "That's all right, Jose," he added with a mischievous grin, "Mature men are best!"

I thought that if Duggan was being subjected to similar intimations, and knowing Jock this seemed not unlikely, meeting, as we inevitably would in our respective jobs, could be embarrassing. As it happened, although I had caught glimpses of a broad shouldered tweed clad figure seated beside Jock in his van, or driving a small blue truck round the dairies, we did not actually meet for nearly two weeks. I had loaded up my sack of cake one morning at the granary and was about to drive away when I saw his little blue truck blocking my access to the road. There was no sign of its driver. Then his head appeared over the door of a loose box.

"Good morning!" he called. "I've got a cow calving here. It may be a bit difficult. Will you give me a hand?" I switched off the tractor and joined him and the cow in the box. He had taken off his jacket and was rolling up the sleeve of a beautifully hand tailored shirt. At a quick glance I noted the well cut cord breeches and the much discussed boots; also that he was every bit as handsome as Algie had said. He took a calving rope out of the Gladstone bag he always carried with him and which, in time, earned him the nickname 'Dr. Duggan'. Putting his hand inside the cow he tied the rope to the barely protruding feet of the calf.

"Now pull downwards, but only when she strains," he instructed me. "But I expect you've done this before," he added, perhaps noting my glance of indignation.

"I've been helping Ernest since December," I told him.

"Oh, I beg your pardon," he replied with mock gravity.

The calving was more straight forward than he had anticipated and it was not long before the wet slimy young creature dropped onto the straw.

We waited until the cow began to clean it and it was struggling to its feet, then washed our hands at the yard tap using soap and towel from the doctor's bag.

"Thank you for your help," said Duggan. "I hope it hasn't delayed you too much."

"Oh, I'll make up the time."

I reflected that for once Ernest might be at the Dutch barn first and start loading. I could then use his excuse that I had been calving a cow.

"I'll move my truck out of your way." Duggan got into the little vehicle, then hesitated. "I've got to take another calf to the dairy at King's Somborne tonight," he said. "Would you care to come with me?" I replied that I would. "Fine, I'll pick you up at 6 o'clock." But I was to see him again before then.

I was having trouble with my tractor. Now, few machines were so abused as an old Fordson tractor, probably because it could be held together with baling wire, or fire on only three cylinders, but would still go and still pull a load, whereas the more splendid Massey Harris or David Brown would be in the workshop if the self starter failed to function. For some time the governor, a small rod that controls the speed, had been coming apart on my tractor, with the result that it would suddenly career off, out of control, like a bolting horse. If I was on the trailer when this happened I had to leap into the driving seat and slam my foot on the clutch. I knew that if I slipped or missed my footing I could fall under the load and find myself back in hospital. I told Jock about it many times.

"Och, I must get it seen to…" he said each time and promptly forgot all about it. It happened again that morning soon after I had left Duggan. I had stopped the tractor and was re-connecting the rod when the blue truck roared across the field and stopped beside me.

"That's the most dangerous thing I've ever seen!" Duggan exclaimed getting out.

"I know. Jock's going to get it fixed … sometime," I replied. Without another word he turned on his heel and went back to the truck. "Don't go away!" he called out of the window. Before I had finished feeding he was back, with a new governing rod. In ten minutes he had it fixed and safe. I was impressed to say the least.

At 6 o'clock he called for me, not in the truck but in Jock's van. I was glad that Algie and Geoff were out and that Mrs Collins was gardening on the other side of the house. I knew they were all very curious to know whether I had met Duggan and I was anxious to conceal the fact for as long as possible. No-one saw me get into the van beside him.

"Just be careful of the seat," he warned me. "It's loose." I tested it. There was certainly nothing to prevent it tipping right back. We picked up the calf from Folly Farm and sat it on the floor between my legs. It was not, however, content with this position and decided that it would be more fun to sit on my lap and from there to look out of the window, or alternatively, to lick my face. I was not too keen on nursing a calf, even if it's rear end was clothed in a sack and a struggle ensued as it determinedly clambered up, digging its sharp little hooves into my shins, and I equally determinedly pushed it down. It was seven miles to Kings Somborne and at last the calf tired and settled down on the floor. Duggan and I were able to enjoy a little uninterrupted conversation. He was just telling me about the farm he had worked on at Hay-on-Wye where he had helped to break hunters and, warming to his subject was driving rather fast, when we came to a sudden bend. At the same time the calf made one more attempt to sit on my lap and the seat tipped back. In a moment the calf and I were rolling together on the floor of the van. Duggan stopped on the first piece of straight road and came to my rescue. Then he found a piece of cord and tied the wayward animal to the inside of the van where it remained for the rest of the journey.

"I hope you'll come out with me again," Duggan said on the way home. "Next time without the calf."

I said I would like that.

"Frenchman's Creek is on in Winchester. We could catch the bus at the Rack & Manger after work. Sorry, I haven't a car. I sold my old Alvis before I came down here."

"The bus will do nicely," I replied.

"It can't be tomorrow night," he told me. "With the rest of the local Home Guard I'm guarding Micheldever tunnel."

"All night?" I asked.

"From 10 o'clock till 5 am."

Algie, too, was on tunnel guard. Next morning he came down to breakfast yawning, tousle headed and bleary eyed.

"What a night!" he groaned. "Cold and damp," he shuddered at the recollection. "Two hours on and two off."

"Was there no shelter?" I asked.

"Oh, a little hut. But every two hours we were woken up and turned out. The only one who remained cheerful all the time was Duggan. You'd have thought he was enjoying it!"

On my round that morning I saw a couple of sleepy eyed tractor drivers, but when I met Duggan at one of the dairies he looked as bright eyed and debonair as if he had spent the whole night in his bed.

"Aren't you missing your sleep?" I asked.

"Not a bit," he replied. "It was good fun!"

Was he really that much more resiliant than his companions of the night watch, I wondered, or just spoofing.

At 5.30 that evening I met him opposite the Rack and Manger in time to catch the Blue Empress into Winchester for the pictures. This gallant old single-decker bus, once royal blue, stopped there three times a day to pick up local people. No-one was ever left behind and on a Saturday she was filled to over capacity. Passengers stood shoulder to shoulder along the deck, others crowded onto the step as, down on her springs, steam belching from the radiator, she chugged and panted up the hill from the pub.

At the end of the afternoon as I finished cutting kale in the field behind the house I had seen the Blue Empress moving slowly along the winding lanes from Kings Somborne, like a bluebottle crawling across a landscape painting. I still followed her progress from my bedroom window as I changed to go out, and I knew I had time to grab a quick cup of tea and a slice of cake and still be at the corner when she throbbed to a brake screeching halt. I could no longer conceal from those interested where I was going, and with whom, nor did they conceal their nods and smiles of satisfaction.

It was an enjoyable film but long, and we missed the Blue Empress on her last trip back to Crawley. On the five-mile walk home we talked mainly, at first, of horses. Duggan had helped to break and train pedigree Shires in Shropshire as well as hunters in Herefordshire, and had hunted regularly with the Hereford and Radnor Border Hounds. Then he recounted some of his early days as a farm pupil, and I, a few of my adventures in the Land Army. He told me about his young brother, a Captain in the Royal Artillery with the 8th army and a sister who was matron of the 9th General Hospital in Malta. Then the conversation changed to books and poetry and we discovered mutual favourites. We covered a mile or two with Keats and Rupert Brooke, and in the company of Houseman we reached the farmhouse gate. After that, we met whenever work allowed and walked in the forestry plantations that surrounded the village or took the Blue Empress into Winchester and strolled along the river to St. Cross.

Meanwhile, my job with the cattle was coming to an end. Most of the cows had calved and joined their respective bails and dairies. The young stock was put on fresh pasture and there was no further need for feeding.

"There's no need for you to worry," said Algie when I expressed my fears of redundancy. "You'll still be needed. I can find plenty of work for you on the arable."

So once again I changed my job, but this time without moving.

CHAPTER 15

Wedding Bells

My work with the arable staff mainly consisted of gang jobs, cleaning out the barns ready for storing the hay and straw of the coming season, and acres of potato planting.

I usually worked with the same group of men. They were Fred and Tom, the senior members of the staff, Maurice, a young married man who lived with his family in one of the Rack and Manger cottages, Norman, a young cousin of Algie's, teenage Dennis, whose lusty and perpetual rendering of "Maresedotes and Doesedotes" rose above the roar of his tractor, and Jesse Lane, a tall, auburn haired, pleasant young man whose name, I thought, was reminiscent of a character in a Western. It was on the pillion of Jesse's motorbike that I travelled to and fro from work, which saved me from the less comfortable journey standing in the back of Algie's or Geoff's truck which was overloaded with men.

The war was now entering its final phase and with other girls working on the land I began to wonder what I should do when it was all over. Like many others, I would not want to return to a town life and job.

In 1942 a WLA Benevolent Fund had been founded with a gift from HM Treasury of £10,000. It was registered as a War Charity and the following year received a personal gift from HM the King. Its purpose was to help girls in need owing to accident or illness. Now it was proposed to fund grants for courses at Agricultural Colleges to further girls' careers in farming or horticulture.

I mentioned this to Duggan one evening as we strolled by the river. His reply was prompt. There was no need for me to worry about that, he said, for by the time the war was over I would be married to him.

"I've loved you since that first day we calved a cow together," he continued, before I could speak. "You're such a funny little thing!"

I hoped there might be other reasons for his affection, but I supposed there was something to be said for keeping one's partner amused.

"I made up my mind then that I was going to marry you."

Do I have any say in this?" I asked politely.

"Well, of course, but I think we can make a go of it, don't you?"

I thought so too. I had not forgotten Richard, and maybe the magic of first love can never be recaptured, but this second time around could be more enduring.

We became engaged before May was out, when we had known each other just two months.

Duggan said that there was no need to wait until the end of the war. We would get married as soon as there was a cottage vacant on the farm and he would talk to the boss about it right away. I was now accustomed to him moving with a speed that had at first taken my breath away. But life was not all river walks and romance. Hay making had come round once more. On this farm the hay was baled straight from the field. Working on the baler was no-one's favourite job. The reason for this became quite clear to me when I sat on the machine as it was drawn with a slow, undulating motion behind the tractor, pushing lengths of stiff oily wire into little holes in an iron bar while Tom sat on the opposite side, tying them. I soon discovered that gloves were necessary to protect my hands and goggles to prevent my eyes becoming perpetually bloodshot and red rimmed from the dust and flying hay seeds. These protective items became sweaty and uncomfortable in the hot sun. At the end of the day hundreds of oblong bales lay in rows across the field to be loaded onto trailers and stacked into ricks or barns. Then came the pleasanter job of taking trailer loads to the Home farm with my old Fordson tractor.

We were haymaking on D-day. For days previously lorries packed with soldiers had passed in continuous cavalcade along the road to Winchester and the coast. Sometimes I sat on my tractor for half-an-hour watching them pass and waiting for an opportunity to cross with my load.

On the day before D-day, bomber drawn gliders carried other troops to drop into Europe. While these dramatic and history-making events were taking place we could only pursue the quiet and commonplace routine of our daily lives. By the time the last hay bale had been stacked away the winter barley was ready for cutting. I was somewhat surprised that combine harvesters were not used on this large acreage of cereal crops. This year the boss was going to experiment with threshing the corn straight from the field, but first it had to be cut with binders.

One sultry afternoon, when the temperature was well into the 70s, I rode the binder behind old Fred on his tractor. Perched on the high iron seat, watching the sheaves drop out onto the stubble and listening to the monotonous rumble and clack of the machine, I grew more and more sleepy.

"Finding it hard to keep awake?" asked Fred, when we stopped once to adjust the tying of the sheaves. "Norman went to sleep on the tractor yesterday and drove clean into the corn."

But I was soon fully awakened by the shrill screaming of a rabbit caught in the knife of the binder. It was impossible to see them crouching in the thick, standing corn and this happened several times during the afternoon. Fred could only jump from the tractor and dispatch them with all possible speed. After tea Algie drove into the field to shoot the last ones as they bolted from the small square of standing corn left in the middle. The shocked sheaves dried quickly in the heat of the following sun filled days and soon the threshing drum was in the field driven by a belt from Dennis's big International tractor. The men unloaded the sheaves from the trailers into the drum while I worked at a girl's usual task of clearing the cavings. When the straw was ready to pick up I was back on the baler again. The weather held for several weeks, with six-and-a-half working days and six evenings in each.

Duggan and I saw each other very little, except for a brief wave as my tractor passed his truck somewhere on the roads round the farm. He had by now met Catherine and won her instant approval, and on several Sunday evenings we had supper at her home. At the end of July a cottage became vacant on the farm.

One evening when rain had stopped harvesting we went to look at it. Standing at the top of the village, below the wood, it had four good-sized rooms, a scullery, and a bathroom converted from a wash-house on the other side of a small concrete yard. A long kitchen garden stretched down to a field.

I closed my eyes to the somewhat tasteless decoration, the shabby paintwork and the water that lay in a pool inside the back door. I would, I thought, feel at home working in gum boots.

"It looks a bit dingy, I know," said Duggan, "but the boss says he'll have repairs done and the whole place redecorated as soon as the workmen have finished the new grain store."

I looked out of the wide window of the front downstairs room, onto a pretty thatched cottage with its colourful garden and a little further up the road, the grey stone of the 12th century church glimpsed through a screen of ancient yews.

"Anyway, it'll do for a start, won't it?" Duggan asked. Once it was decorated to our own taste it would do very nicely I thought. We began to think about furnishing and to delve into the complications of permits and coupons for furniture, floor covering, bed linen and curtains. We discovered that our permits allowed us a suite for the bedroom or the dining room, so we had the choice of sleeping on the floor or eating off it. We decided to try the second hand shops. In a back street behind the square in Winchester Duggan discovered what appeared to be, from the outside, a junk shop, but in the dark recesses at the back there were some good pieces of furniture. It was owned by an old couple. The wife, taciturn and tight lipped, was clearly the boss. In time she took a motherly interest in us – especially in Duggan. Each time he had an errand into Winchester for one of the dairies he would visit the shop to find that she had something put on one side that she thought would interest him. There was a small, heavy oak, gate-legged table, and later four carved oak, wicker-backed chairs which he bought and loaded up in the back of his truck or Jock's van together with the farm purchases. A little mahogany desk, reproduction Sheraton, shared transport with some cartons of worming powders and boxes of fencing nails. Similarly an armchair travelled with a roll of barb wire and its pair, a few days later, with a tarpaulin. These Duggan unloaded at the cottage and in the evening when I had finished work I met him there to see the latest purchases.

By the time the wheat was cut on the farm we were well on the way to getting a home together. We had talked to the vicar and fixed the wedding date for the 16th September at 8am, to give us time to reach Aberystwyth, where we were spending the first few days of our honeymoon, by the evening. Because both our families were so far away, with the exception of my mother, Dai, the farm mechanic and a fellow Welshman was to be Duggan's best man, while Jock had consented to give me away.

We spent Sunday afternoons at the cottage, arranging furniture; hanging temporary curtains and a few hunting prints; putting out books and photographs; unpacking wedding presents and writing letters. But these were only a few hours in a week where every daylight hour was filled by the major task of harvest.

Hundreds of acres of cut wheat lay to the north of the farm, on the downs toward Stockbridge. I was alternatively on jobs of shocking or threshing or carting straw bales to the barns. With the last job we had help from several black GIs from a camp near the village. They were willing, hard-working and capable of amazing feats of physical strength. One nineteen-year-old, tall and slim with Harry Bellafonte looks, whose name was Henry, continually rode the wing of my tractor to and from the field. One evening at dusk, as we were returning with a last load, the draw pin broke and tractor and trailer parted company. The well loaded bales did not fall but I thought with dismay of having to unload them in order to lift the drawbar and fasten it again, with a new pin, to the tractor. I looked at Henry.

"No problem," he said with a shrug of his broad shoulders. Walking nonchalantly over to the load he lifted the drawbar with the weight of some eighty bales behind it, held it while I backed the tractor and dropped in the pin. Then, without any sign of exertion he climbed back onto the tractor wing.

"I'm glad I had you along!" I said.

The evenings were drawing in. It was getting dark at 8.30 as I hitched off the trailer, put on the tractor headlights and in top gear, sped homeward through the lanes. The beam of light aroused cockchafers from the grass. Bumbling and confused after their long day underground, they flew into my face and hair. Although I knew that they were harmless I did not care for their furry bodies and hard wings at such close quarters. I liked them even less when they came into my room at night and noisily power dived my pillow like miniature aircraft. I closed the windows firmly only to find that they came down the chimney. Mrs Collins obligingly stuffed this up with newspaper to keep them out, but their frantic buzzing when they became trapped in the paper was just as prohibitive to sleep. The men called them pin-shavers or more recently, doodle-bugs, their name for the V-1 rockets which made a similar throbbing drone as they passed overhead. We were all apprehensive of this latest wartime threat.

"Tis all right when ee 'ears 'em," said old Harry the rabbit catcher. "Tis when ee don't - then watch out!"

The long spell of fine weather finally broke and we awoke to a morning of heavy rain.

"That's the end of harvesting for a bit," said Algie, looking out of the window after breakfast. "There are some trailer loads of bales to be unloaded in the barn at the Home Farm. Lucky thing we got them all in last night and covered them over. Perhaps you could give the men a hand, Jose. I'll run you up there."

I was grateful that he had not suggested that I went on my bike and that I was going to have a job in the dry – or that is what I thought; the Home Farm Dairy herd, however, determined otherwise. It was just the sort of morning when cows will decide to get into some forbidden field. This time the ideal choice from their point of view was the six foot high maize. Once in, they were not coming out in a hurry. With Algie, Jesse, Norman and Dennis I walked up and down behind them, urging them to the ends of the long rows, in the still torrential rain, getting an extra douching from the long pointed leaves that were well above my head. It took half-an-hour to get the last of the cows out of the field and hand them over to the cowmen who had conveniently been at breakfast during this little episode.

Algie looked at me with a slow amused smile as I stood, dripping, by his van.

"Jump in," he said, "I'll take you home and you may as well have the rest of the day off."

There was just time to dry and change and catch the Blue Empress into Winchester. This was indeed an opportunity to do some much needed shopping.

Duggan drew up in his truck as I waited for the bus. He had been to town the day before, he told me, to collect something from the vet, and had picked up from the station a bed and a chest of linen sent from his home.

"There's a jolly nice eiderdown," he added. "Great," I said, "Then we won't have to sleep on the floor or take old Harry's advice with regard to bed covering!"

"Yer wants t' do wot me an' t' Missus did last winter" Harry had told us with the air of one divulging a piece of valuable advice.

"Get a couple of wheat sacks, sew 'em together an' fill 'em with straw. That'll keep you warm a treat."

Armed with all available cash and coupons I was going to look for saucepans, crockery and curtain material.

"Do you think you can choose it yourself?" Duggan asked. It was he who had done most of the home buying so far and he seemed doubtful of my capabilities in anything that did not relate to the farm. Perhaps he was right. As a potential housewife I was a very good tractor driver and I doubted whether my expertise at putting up bales or backing a tractor and loaded trailer accurately at any angle through gateways and barn doors would help much when it came to coping with the baked and boiled.

I had acquired two books, one entitled *Teach Yourself to Cook*, another on *Hints for the Housewife*, with a third *The Technique of Sex* lent to me by Catherine, They rubbed shoulders with old favourites such as a Keats Anthology A. G. Street's *Farmer's Glory* and the *Fordson Tractor Manual*. Incidentally, Duggan did approve, after all, of the glazed chintz with a spring floral design that I had chosen for curtains. I also proved myself capable of buying saucepans. Curiously the purchase that pleased me most was a perfectly ordinary brown coffee pot. It is strange today to remember what commonplace things were practically unobtainable at the end of 1944 and what new homemakers were pleased to make use of. From corn sacks of good quality hessian, washed and dyed, I covered seats of kitchen chairs and made matching curtains, while calf milk bags, dyed or bleached, provided tea towels, chair backs and cushion covers. Many a bride went to the altar dressed in parachute silk. My own wedding outfit was to be an appropriate mixture of old, new and borrowed, namely a pre-war suit of natural shantung which had seen little wear during my Land Army years, a new blouse and a matching hat borrowed from Dai's wife, Megan.

Although Duggan and I had no extra time off because of our impending marriage, and had asked for none, both managers sympathetically contrived to give us time together whenever it was possible. So when a spare part was needed for a binder from an agricultural engineers near Marlborough, Algie suggested to the boss that Duggan should be sent to fetch it, and in case he needed a navigator to find the place, that I should go with him in that capacity. So on a Saturday afternoon we drove across the Wiltshire Downs in his little truck. Fresh winds had dispersed the rain clouds, the cleared acres of stubble looked washed and bright and the blue sky was broken by massed cumulus clouds like mountain ranges. We collected the part and had tea in the ancient city of Marlborough, driving home as the sun set in a crimson glow behind the hills.

The men, who had been working all through the long, hot afternoon seemed not to begrudge us these few hours of freedom. Rather, they were as pleased as we were that this brief interlude had been arranged. Duggan, in his short time at the farm, had become very popular with the staff except for the difficult few who had subsequently experienced his explosive Welsh temper and found him a formidable person to cross.

After the rain, corn threshing from the field was abandoned and the last fields of spring wheat were ricked. Tom built the ricks with Fred and me passing the sheaves to him as they dropped from the elevator. All day Dennis, Norman and Jesse brought in loads from the field. When we reached the roof Fred got down and I passed the sheaves to Tom as he put them carefully into place, then I, too, left him and he stood in a small hole in the side of the roof placing the last sheaves.

My final two weeks in the Land army were spent on this same job. When it came to the last morning and I arrived at the field on the pillion of Jesse's motorbike, Tom took me by the arm. "Now as this is your last day I'm going to let you build the rick," he said, with the air of one promising a child some rare treat. I laughed, thinking that this was more of the leg-pulling that I was constantly subjected to.

"I mean it. You've been watching me for two weeks. It's time you could do it. I'll mark it out for you. Then you'll be on your own."

So as the loads came in I placed the sheaves as I had seen Tom do and Will Prangle years before, keeping the sides straight and level and building up the corners. At dinner time the men walked round the rick, criticising its construction.

"Struth, don't stand underneath it you!" said one. "It's like to go over any minute!"

"I wouldn't rate its chances in a high wind," agreed another.

"Don't you pay no heed to they," Tom encouraged me, "You'm doin' all right."

By early afternoon we had started on the roof and the third helper got down, leaving Tom and me working together until, towards evening, he descended the ladder and I was left standing in a little nest at the top of the elevator to finish the ridge, then, with the very last sheaves to fill in the hole around me. By now the rick seemed as high as a house and I would be glad to get down. Two men wheeled away the elevator and I waited for them to put up the ladder in its place. But instead they walked resolutely away and got on their tractors. Gradually it dawned on me that they had no intention of getting me down.

"We'll tell your fiance where you are. If he wants you he can come and get you!" called cheeky young Dennis. I appealed to Jesse, but he started up his motor bike and roared off across the stubble. I looked for Tom. Surely he would not let them do this to me. He was riding on a trailer, apparently having some trouble with lighting his pipe. So the tractors filed out through the field gate and the sound of their engines and clattering trailers slowly died away, leaving me to the silence of the September dusk. I wriggled into a more comfortable position among the sheaves to wait. How long, I wondered, would they keep up their little joke?

Somewhere a clock struck eight; at that same time the next morning I was to be married. There were just twelve hours to transform a tired, grubby, work-worn Land Girl into some semblance of a radiant bride. Five minutes or so passed. Screech owls called from the wood and a few pipistrelle bats wheeled and dived about my head. Then in the distance I heard a motor-cycle returning. A few minutes later it turned in at the gate. With all the aplomb of a gallant knight rescuing a fair lady, Jesse leapt from his iron steed, put up the ladder and steadied it as I climbed down.

"You didn't really think we'd leave you up there?" he asked sheepishly as I climbed gratefully onto the pillion, glancing back just once with pride at my rick; it matched its fellows and would stand through the winter. Then my thoughts turned to a hot bath and sleep. But the day was not yet over.

As we neared the farm buildings we saw black smoke rising above the trees.

"Folly Barn's on fire!" Jesse yelled over his shoulder as he swerved into the yard.

A number of men were fighting the blaze with buckets of water from the dairy. It seemed that Dennis had been refuelling his tractor with the engine running when a spark from the exhaust had ignited the fuel, which in turn had set fire to the thatched roof of the barn The boss, who was directing operations pounced on Jesse and me.

"You two – there are some good bales of hay in that barn. Get them out!"

Luckily there were not many but they were at the far end of the building and we staggered to and fro dodging falling lumps of burning thatch. Briefly I envisaged a heading in the local paper 'Land Girl burned on eve of wedding', then dismissed it as over-dramatising the situation. A vibrant clanging bell announced the arrival of the fire engine. Somehow Duggan, who was among the fire-fighters, managed to get possession of a hose and was finding it hard to control. "Play it onto the roof from inside," he shouted to the fireman behind him, always in his element in a crisis, but before they could raise it the boss came in at the other door to be met with the full jet of water in the middle of his ample person. He was a difficult target to miss and as he dodged to one side, so Duggan followed him with a second douching.

He took it with extreme good nature under the circumstances. Not until the fire was out and the men had dispersed did he attempt verbal retaliation.

"You won't be able to get married tomorrow Duggan" he joked. "The parson's gone up in flames!"

It was dark when Duggan eventually dropped me at our cottage where I was spending the night. My mother, who had arrived during the afternoon, was getting increasingly anxious at my non-appearance.

"You don't look much like a bride, darling," she remarked, looking in dismay at my hands and face where black and smuts from the fire were smeared over the usual layer of harvest dust, and at my eyes red rimmed from the smoke.

"Oh, a bath and a night's sleep will work wonders," I replied.

I washed my hair, then soaked in hot water to which I had added the last of some precious bath salts. I gave special attention to my hands so that the one I presented to Duggan in the morning would not resemble that of a seasoned farm labourer. By the time I emerged from the bathroom Mummy had prepared a meal from provisions she had thoughtfully brought with her.

"I didn't think you would have any food in the house, dear," she said.

How right she was. Clean and fed I felt a lot better. Sleep would do the rest. But after we had talked for a while and I had packed my case for the morning it was nearly midnight.

As I drew back the curtains before getting into bed I saw that the heavy cloud which had prevailed for the past few days had cleared away and the moon shone brightly – tomorrow was going to be a lovely day.

CHAPTER 16

A Farmer's Wife

I awoke at 6.30am to a perfect September morning. The sky
was cloudless blue behind a thin veil of mist; the dew spangled
garden reflected a pink shrouded sunlight.

After a light breakfast with my mother we prepared
refreshments for the few wedding guests. It was very much a
wartime repast. No wedding cake or champagne, just
sandwiches and coffee. I was dressed and ready when Jock
arrived at twenty minutes to eight. He looked me up and
down with approval.

"Aye, Ah reckon you'll do," he remarked.

My mother preceded me to the church and at five-to-eight
the hired car arrived from Winchester, a big old Austin driven
by a pretty, curly-haired young woman who took us the few
yards to the church. Still too early, we walked up and down
the long, gravel path between the pitted, lichen covered
tombstones and the dark, spreading yews. At 8 o'clock exactly
we stood in the porch. I must have been the most punctual
bride on record! From the doorway I could see Duggan with
Dai beside him, seated in the front pew. My mother, Vi and
Megan made up the congregation. But where was the vicar?
He was not in the church, nor was his car outside. Was he ill?
Had he forgotten? Or had he, as the boss had facetiously
suggested, perished in last night's fire? Five minutes passed;
ten. Duggan turned round anxiously, then conferred with Di.

Vi and Megan whispered together, My mother fidgeted. It was 8.15. Our train left at 9 o'clock. Even observing strict punctuality we had a very narrow margin of time.

Now the chances of catching it were diminishing with every minute.

"How can he be so late?" I sighed.

"Aye, he's wuss than blodd auld Ernest," muttered the incorrigible Jock. Just then the vicar emerged from the vestry and took his place on the chancel steps.

When at last I stood beside Duggan and the service began, we forgot trains and time and our previous anxiety at the late arrival of the vicar (we learned afterward that he had been unable to start his car), even if we did leave the church with somewhat irreverent haste. Running down the path, we got into the waiting car, waving briefly to two women, cowmen's wives, who were watching by the lych gate.

"Do you think you can make it?" we asked our driver.

"I'll do my best," she replied doubtfully. We dived into the house, changed hastily, grabbed our suitcases and, waving "goodbye" to our guests, we were away – almost. Half way through the village Duggan suddenly put his hand to his breast pocket.

"I've come without my wallet!" he exclaimed. Slowly and with difficulty our driver turned the long car in the narrow street, while the cowmen's wives who had followed us, waved their arms in gestures of protest.

"You can't turn back. It's terrible bad luck!" they cried, "You mustn't turn back!"

"It'll be more unlucky if I go without any money," said Duggan. I remained in the car while it turned once again. We were well on the way to Winchester when Duggan remembered that he had not packed his shaving tackle or brought his pipe and I thought of those sandwiches put ready for our journey. But there was no more turning back.

The train left ten minutes before we arrived at the booking office. There was another, a slow, stopping train, in fifteen minutes. This meant that we would miss our connection at Crewe. It was going to be a long day. We sat down disconsolately on the platform seat, where we were joined a moment later by none other than Ernest, off to visit his brother at Fleet. Duggan seemed delighted to see him and they settled down right away to a cosy little chat about the milk yields at various dairies and a suspected case of mastitis, followed by a friendly argument about some calving dates over which their opinions differed.

My brief period of limelight as a bride was over. I sat forlorn and forgotten on the edge of the seat, suddenly relegated to that normal status of a farmer's wife – second to the cow. I attempted to divert myself by watching other passengers, wondering whether the two Land Girls on the edge of the platform were going home or to fresh jobs and what they would do after the war. Perhaps they, too, would soon marry a farmer or farm worker. Immediately in front of us was a tall, slender WAAF officer with pretty legs, but nothing could distract Duggan and Ernest from their conversation.

"Then there's that milk fever case at Bail 5," Ernest was saying. At last our train chugged its way into the station, and with a belch of steam came to a halt. Duggan seemed not to notice. The WAAF with the good legs was already on the train, the Land Girls were climbing into a carriage when the dairy experts finished sorting out the milk fever case and got up.

"Well, all the best to you," said Ernest, "and to the Missus."

Duggan remembered me then. Turning to pick up the cases, he smiled.

"Come along then ... Missus."

Duggan.

APPENDIX

After The Land Army

When, in the autumn of 1944, I returned my uniform, covered over my tractor for the last time and left the ranks of the Women's Land Army to become one of Britain's housewives, the change was as complete and bewildering as that from hotel receptionist to farm worker over four years earlier.

Duggan left the house at 7am, returning an hour later for breakfast, leaving me confronted by unfamiliar tasks which proved full of pitfalls for the uninitiated: porridge that boiled over; toast and bacon that burned while I coaxed an unwilling fire. Then there was the weekly wash. On farms I had handled heavy machinery and large animals but I took off my Land Army hat to the little woman who could hang out a flapping, wet sheet without tripping over it or trailing it in the mud! As I tried to concoct an appetising meal from our meagre rations with a wartime recipe book propped up before me, it was not without a tinge of nostalgia that I glimpsed a tractor's progress in a distant field.

But even if I no longer ploughed, I still dug for victory in our cottage garden and also worked part time on the farm during the potato harvest.

Our first Christmas was saddened by the loss of Duggan's much-loved younger brother, a Captain in the Royal Artillery, who was killed in Italy in the last week of the campaign while serving as Observation Officer.

In May there were celebrations in the village street and at the Fox and Hounds at the end of hostilities with Germany and again in September when the war finally ended with 'VJ day'.

By this time we were embarking on our first move. For Duggan to acquire experience and advancement in farm management we moved frequently during the early days of our marriage. Our first son was born in Oxfordshire, the second in Somerset, the third in Hampshire, then ten years later I produced our fourth in my native Sussex. Duggan was then managing a thousand acre mixed farm with a three thousand acre shoot near Chichester plus another thousand acres on the Downs near Midhurst.

Life was busy for me too with the care of a large 18th Century farmhouse and garden, the family, horses, dogs and village commitments – of which Duggan also had a large share – and my absorbing hobby of writing and publishing local history.

After 27 years on this farm Duggan retired and we moved to a small bungalow near the village with a large cultivated garden and extensive wild garden which prevented me suffering withdrawal symptoms from farm life and provided ample playground for visiting grandchildren.

Our interest in farming continued, and even more so in the environment and wildlife, interests which began for me, fifty years ago in my 'Corduroy Days'.

In 1990, while Duggan and I were spending a week in Brockenhurst, I met Richard, who in retirement was again living in the New Forest with his wife. In the following years the four of us became good friends.

Duggan died in 1995, a year after our Golden Wedding. I live on at the cottage, taking part in church and village activities and spending time with my now large family, but perhaps I am never happier than when in the garden, working the soil or tidying and coppicing in my bit of woodland.

I am, after all, still a Land Girl at heart.

Josephine Duggan Rees
April 2000

The author, at home in the garden in 1999.

The Women's Land Army was disbanded on November 30th 1950, by which time some girls had worked on the land for over ten years.

For a number of them and for others whose service was of shorter duration the experience changed the course of their lives.